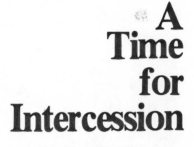

A
Time
for
Intercession

Erwin Prange

Creation House
Carol Steam, Illinois

Published by Creation House, 499 Gundersen Drive,
Carol Stream, Illinois, 60187
In Canada: Beacon Distributing Ltd., 104 Consumers Drive,
Whitby, Ontario L1N 5T3
In Australia: Oracle Australia, Ltd., 18-26 Canterbury Road,
Heathmont, Victoria 135

Biblical quotations from the *New American Standard Bible*
© 1971 are used with permission from the Lockman Foundation.

ISBN 0-88419-004-8
Library of Congress Catalog Card Number 76-20085
Printed in the United States of America

CONTENTS

FOREWORD

It is not easy to come up with a fresh, original word on the theme of prayer. Erv Prange has done it.

This is a book about God—and people. So thoroughly grounded in Scripture, yet so rich in human experience, that in the best sense of the phrase it is a handbook of intercession.

Some things in this book may shock you. Some will amuse you. Some may well move you to tears. It is not a book of sweet platitudes. When he writes, "We keep on praying until the Lord says, Yes, No, or Shutup," well, you know that Erv Prange is more interested in being practical than pious. He *tells* you how in simple, clearly stated principles, then he *shows* you how from real life situations. He makes intercession exciting.

Clearly this is a book that has grown out of life, not out of research in libraries. When he speaks about patterns of intercession, praying the family covenant, or marriage healing, you sense that what he says comes out of a life and ministry truly taught of the Holy Spirit.

"The intercessor on his knees is the channel for God's healing love to a broken world," he tells us. "We are not mere spectators at the drama of creation, redemption and healing, but partners with God through intercession." The challenge of that partnership will come alive as you read this book.

Larry Christenson

INTRODUCTION

It happened toward the end of our regular Friday night healing service. A member of a neighboring church and her daughter had come to the altar to stand in proxy for their son and grandson, who was dying from an undiagnosed disease. We had prayed together many times before about this.

Several times the son had come and we had talked and prayed. Always we seemed to receive an assurance that God wanted to heal. Yet, the more we prayed the worse he seemed to become. All of us were in a state of confusion and semi-despair.

That night as the neighbor and her daughter knelt before me on the outside of the communion rail, I paused and we meditated a few moments in silence. Finally, I said, "Lord, I don't know what is blocking this healing. I don't know how to pray in this situation. Please give me Your words, please give me a prayer that's right in the center of Your will and love. Give me the prayer of the Intercessor, Himself."

9

As I laid my hands on the neighbor's head a strange kind of prayer came forth. I heard myself saying, "Lord, take me instead; don't take this young man. He hasn't lived his life; he has young children; he isn't ready to go. I've lived my life, I think I'm ready to go." Then, later, the words of Spurgeon came to me, "God's man is immortal till his task is done."

The next morning my telephone buzzed. The neighbor was extremely agitated. "Don't you ever pray like that for me again! I didn't sleep a wink all last night."

"Why, what's the matter? What did I do now?" I asked innocently.

"The very idea of offering your life for my grandson! He isn't worth it. We aren't worthy. Your life is so much more important to God and man than his. Never, never pray like that again! It scares me."

"But," I protested, "you don't understand. That's the prayer of the intercessor. That's the heart of the Gospel. There was nothing high or heroic about it. I just don't place that high a value on my life."

In Isaiah 59, the Lord looked for an intercessor and could find none. Then Isaiah 53 says that Jesus poured out his soul in death and made intercession for the transgressors. "If we are going to pray in the name and in the manner of Jesus, then we will have to be intercessors," I reminded her.

"Well, I don't understand all that. I know that you care a lot, you pray for a lot of people, but don't you ever dare offer your life for my grandson again."

Next day I preached about intercession. I tried to explain to the congregation that this was the core of the Gospel, the prayer from the cross. Jesus is always saying the same thing, "Father, don't punish them, punish me. Don't look at them, look at me. Don't take them, take me. Let me take their place. Let me suffer, die and pay for their sin."

And then He is saying, "Father, when they pray, don't look at them, don't listen to them, look at me, listen to me, I am the head of the Body." Then in the sermon I tried to explain that Jesus' unlimited prayer promises, "Whatever you ask the Father in my name," were tied in with the role of the intercessor. I related my encounter with the neighbor as an example.

Strangely, I got almost the same reaction from the congregation. An even stronger reaction came from my family. They were all saying, "Well, fine, but what about us? Do you have a right to offer up your life? Does it really belong to you alone? What about your congregation? What about your family and children? What about the people that you minister to?"

I thought about this a great deal. And I wondered sometimes if it wasn't the way Jesus' family and the disciples also approached Him. After He had revealed His destiny to the inner core of the disciples, Peter said, "Lord, we're not going to let You do it!"

Jesus then replied, "Get behind me, Satan!" The whole concept of the intercessor began to open up. How was God's governing of the world and the church tied up with intercession? Was there a secret here that we had overlooked?

The thought was not a new one. It actually began more than thirty years before, during World War II. I was overseas, stationed in England. Because I spoke flawless German, I worked with G-5 and G-2. During the next five years, I saw a lot of strange and unbelievable things. Either Hitler was crazy or we were just lucky. Perhaps God really was on our side.

It began with the Dunkirk evacuation, which happened before we landed in England. When we got there and heard the true story, I could scarcely believe it. Why did the German army suddenly pull back for a few hours and give the British Expeditionary Force time to assemble on the beach? The wild, choppy

11

English Channel was like a lake of glass that day, so that even rowboats could cross.

Then came the Battle of Britain. I witnessed part of that. Why did Germany break off the Battle of Britain? The last British fighter plane was on the ground. At the very moment when the Battle of Britain was won for Germany, and England could have been had for the taking, suddenly the Germans turned away toward the Mediterranean Sea.

What about the Normandy invasion? On that day, one day after my 27th birthday, the greatest armada ever assembled in history crossed the English Channel. Not a single German plane or submarine opposed the crossing. For the next thirty days the weather was so bad, it would have been impossible to mount an invasion.

If the Normandy invasion had not taken place when it did, the V-2s would surely have wiped out Britain. I was in England when the V-2s began to fall. It was eerie. One would be walking along a quiet city street and suddenly, right in front of your eyes, a whole block would erupt into the air. As the debris disintegrated and exploded, a tremendous detonation would occur, and finally a concussion that often knocked one to the ground.

There were other mysteries and absurdities that I just couldn't fit together. One of them was the battle for Africa. The Afrikorps was undoubtedly one of the most professional armies ever fielded in modern warfare. General Erwin Rommel, whose son I was to meet personally right after the war, was perhaps the greatest general on both sides of the war. Then, right at the gates of Cairo, when victory was in their grasp, the mighty Afrikorps surrendered.

Later on, we discovered that the British had set up an eight-inch water line for fresh water. It had just been completed the day before. On that day they were testing it for three hours with salt water because fresh water was too precious. During those three hours the Germans broke through. They shot the line full of holes and began thirstily to gulp down the salt water, not realizing what it was.

In the hot desert sun, where the temperatures ran as high as 120 degrees in the shade, they were immediately immobilized. With black tongues hanging out, they gasped for air and life. They threw down their weapons and put up their hands in surrender. The gate of Cairo remained closed. The Bible lands were saved.

What utter folly and madness prompted Hitler to attack Russia? After his initial success, when he could have walked into Moscow without firing a shot, he turned aside and the mighty German army committed suicide in Stalingrad. After the plan had been formulated for the attack on Russia, it was delayed for a vital two weeks while Hitler quelled a revolt in the Balkans. These two weeks proved to be fatal, for they allowed the Russians to defeat Hitler as they had Napoleon.

Other questions puzzled me. War was so terrible, such utter madness, that no one ever really won. One side just seemed to lose more than the other.

But how did God fit into all this insanity? Whose side was He really on? Neither? Or both? How did He feel about all this cruel bloodshed and pain? Why was He silent over Dachau, Buchenwald and the frigid Siberian death camps? What about the holocaust that almost wiped out His people? How did God involve Himself in this bloody tragedy called History? Did He care? Did He have a higher plan? This was the question that had to be answered as the fullness of the Spirit unfolded in my life, beginning with December 7, 1963.

In 1973, while I was a pastor in Baltimore, a friend of

mine gave me a book, *Rees Howells, Intercessor,* by Norman Grubb. As I read it, and especially as I neared the end, chills ran up and down my body. Here was the key, a partial answer at least, to that great mystery ... *how does God involve Himself in human destiny?*

The book tells how in 1939, when Hitler began to take over all of Europe, Rees Howells, a Welsh coal-miner/evangelist, had a word from the Lord. The word was that Hitler would be defeated. He repeated this word, perhaps prematurely, so that it appeared in various headlines.

Soon after publication of this prophecy, Hitler began to take over all of Europe and Howells was labeled a false prophet. But he said, "I know that the Lord has spoken to me; I know that this word is true." And so from that time on, beginning roughly with Dunkirk, Rees Howells gathered together his intercessors. Every night for five years they prayed a self-fulfilling prophecy into reality.

At the time of the Dunkirk evacuation Howells went off alone for three days and three nights. He wrestled with the Lord in a way that left him, like Jacob, limping and a semi-invalid for the rest of his life. As he and his group of intercessors prayed each night, the Holy Spirit began to give them the prayers to pray.

He said, "Pray that Germany will break off the Battle of Britain," and it happened. Then He said, "Pray for the Normandy invasion," and it succeeded against all odds. The Spirit began to speak more and more plainly to the intercessors. At one time, He said, "Pray that Germany will attack Russia, because I am going to judge them both; pray that Germany will not take Moscow but attack Stalingrad instead and be destroyed."

The Spirit then began to reveal a part of the plan. When Germany broke off the Battle of Britain, the intercessors were told that they should pray that the

14

enemy become bogged down in Greece in order that the Bible lands might be saved. When the Afrikorps were at the gates of Cairo, the Spirit said plainly, "Pray that the Bible lands will be kept open and the Afrikorps defeated."

All through the course of the war, the Spirit of God guided these intercessors and through them guided and directed the course and the outcome of the war. It was a tremendous revelation but it also raised an awful lot of questions.

How does God work His mercy in the midst of the tremendous problem of human pain? How does the love and goodness of God interact with evil and tragedy? And finally, how do we cooperate with God most effectively as channels and intercessors? What part do we play in the history of the world and the church?

Some of Norman Grubb's other books describe how one man prayed the Gospel into a whole country. C. T. Studd, his father-in-law, almost single-handedly prayed the Gospel into Africa. Praying Hyde prayed the Gospel into India almost alone. In a manner of speaking, Hudson Taylor prayed the Gospel into China. As Charles Wesley said, "The world has yet to see what one man fully yielded to God might accomplish."

This book is about the unfolding of intercession. It began with my encounter with God in a church in Brooklyn, N.Y., described in a Logos book, *The Gift Is Already Yours*. The unfolding continued through a ministry of healing that gradually broadened to physical, emotional, spiritual, and then total healing. For two and one-half years, we held a healing service every Friday evening.

I made a number of trips to Minneapolis and various other parts of the country, praying for thousands of sick people. Many were healed and many seemed not to be healed, but all the time the Lord was showing me something far deeper and far more important. Sometimes painfully and sometimes gloriously, sometimes slowly and sometimes suddenly, the Lord was unfolding a deeper secret and a greater blessing. The unfolding process is still going on.

Where will it lead? I do not know. The pace is accelerating rapidly. Sometimes, I can barely hang on to God's carousel. And the challenges are becoming greater as I grow old and tired. Many times I want to pray, "Lord, give me the strength to stand my blessings!"

The road has often led through the wilderness. More often than not, it has gone into the depths. God is not always in the center of life but in the margins, in the depths. God is always at the very end of the last road, just beyond the ultimate reaches of our imagination, as we stand on the tiptoes of faith. Yes, God is leading us somewhere and showing us something, something vastly more important and vastly deeper than we can say or think or imagine.

As I look back, the steps seem to be rebirth, renewal, deliverance; physical healing, emotional healing, spiritual healing, healing of relationships and total healing. And from there we move into proxy prayers, the family covenant, and into the concept of the intercessor. Yet, we have only scratched the surface. This is only the beginning. God, where are you taking us?

As I write now, it is from the perspective of associate pastor of one of the largest churches of my denomination on the East Coast. As many as 600 Spirit-filled people may be in this one congregation. Already the Lord is unfolding a tremendous plan to Pastor John Austin and myself. It's a possibility so wonderful and challenging that it frightens both of us. A tremendous anointing upon this congregation defies any rational explanation.

God seems to be saying that He wants to form teaching and renewal centers for His church. We have already begun to enlist our membership in a discipleship program. They will be trained to pray, to witness, to use the Word of God, and to find their individual ministries. The goal of this program is to eradicate that class of church members called pew warmers. We hope to help every member find and enter into his individual ministry. For many that ministry will be intercession.

In the meantime all statistics for growth and expansion of this congregation are running off the map. Material successes and blessings are far beyond our wildest dreams. But, again, there is that intuition of the Spirit that God is leading us into something deeper and more profound.

What is God going to do in this congregation, in the church, in the world? Lord, where are you taking us? As we are swept along to that great divine event toward which the whole creation moves, what are we supposed to be doing? The answer seems to be tied in to the mysterious power of intercession. If there ever was a time for intercession, it is *now*.

1

A TIME FOR INTERCESSION

Lord, we need to grow up to the stature and image of Jesus Christ. That's a long way to go. Help us by Your Spirit to get beyond childish things and not be spiritual babies. Give us a desire for strong meat and wean us from the milk of shallow faith and childish truth.

Jesus, You made intercession for the transgressors and tasted death for every man; make us also channels of Your intercession. Stand before us and make intercession to the Father, in and for and through us. Holy Spirit of God, help us to go out from ourselves and become channels of the resurrection life in the world. Pour out Your ascension gifts on the church through our intercessions.

Lord of the Harvest, we pray for Your harvest. Show us more clearly that all evangelism involves prayer and that every soul is prayed into the kingdom.

Father, You would have all men to be saved; forgive us our neglect of those who are not. Let no soul be lost for our lack of prayer or love. Let Your perfect will in the world be channeled through our prayers. Oh, Jesus, You have no hands and feet or voice in the world except ours; please use us to the fullest.

In Your name and manner we pray.
Amen. Amen. So be it.

The time for burning, for hurting, is past. If we are to survive, now is the time for intercession. In the vital areas of cold war, energy, food, population, pollution, human relations, morals, crime, and many others, we are on a collision course. Some of these areas could reach a crisis point in less than ten years. The question is not *what*, but *when* and *how*?

The world could go out with a tremendous bang in some kind of bimillennial Fourth of July, if nuclear warfare should ever become a reality. Or we could die with a soft whimper by simply running out of everything and choking in our own pollution.

There is still another scenario. That is the direct intervention of God, short of the end of history. This intervention could come in the church and the world. In fact, there are signs that it is already beginning in both areas. Estimates are that as many as ten million people have been renewed by God's Spirit during the past decade.

There are strong hints that some kind of spiritual renewal is brewing inside of vast mother Russia. In spite of all the persecution, repression and atheism, a great Russian writer has said, "Russia is on the verge of a vast spiritual revolution." At the present time the

Spirit is being poured out upon Finland in an unprecedented way. Renewal is leaking over into Russia, and it is estimated that during the past three years as many as a million new Christians have emerged in Siberia alone.

No matter how we write the scenario, we know that we are nearing the end of our human resources. The Golden Age, so boldly proclaimed by the idealists of the nineteenth century, is not likely to happen. Money, prosperity, education, technology—all of these human fables have failed to solve our major problems. In fact, this century, the century of progress, has been the bloodiest of them all. More people have died for the name of Christ in the twentieth century than in all the other nineteen combined.

Perhaps as many as a half billion people have been killed, wounded or displaced by wars in this century alone. The money expended directly or indirectly for war in the twentieth century would buy a four-bedroom, three-bath, two-car-garage home for every family on the face of the earth. What is more, one of the garages could contain a Mercedes Benz and the other a Cadillac Eldorado, all paid for.

The time has come to seek new answers. Certainly the time has come to repent of past sins and admit past mistakes. The bills for the sins and indulgences of our brief history are all suddenly coming due. The party is over in the United States with the disappearance of cheap energy.

The bills for the slave ships are now being collected in the crime-ridden ghettos of our great cities. The notes for our careless wars and prodigal ways are being called in. In Vietnam we saw the limitations of our power; in the energy crisis, the limitations of our wealth; and in Watergate, the limitations of our morality.

It is certainly not the time for complacency or for easy answers. Utopia is dead, Pollyanna has grown up, and the Optimist Club has closed down for repairs. It is a time when all men should think seriously about that ubiquitous sign, "Jesus is the Answer." What does it take to make men realize that there is no meaning or hope outside of God?

The latest projections of the medical profession indicate that one person out of ten in America is heading for acute alcoholism. Every alcoholic affects adversely at least seven other people. Alcohol is beyond doubt the number one drug and social problem in America.

When I was chaplain intern at City Hospital in Baltimore, it seemed to me that the residents of this city were trying to drown themselves in a Chesapeake Bay of alcohol.

"Chaplain, I've been an alcoholic for thirty years. It has destroyed my life, my health, my family and my soul. The doctors say that if I take another drink, I will die. Yet I know exactly what I am going to do when I get out of this hospital."

"What?" I would ask innocently.

"I'm going down to the nearest liquor store or bar."

"But why? It just doesn't make sense. It sounds as if you don't even like alcohol. God wants us to love our enemies, but this is going too far."

"Yes, why? I hate the stuff bitterly. Can you tell me why, Chaplain? Is it me or the devil or even God that makes me drink? One thing I know, I cannot control myself. Chaplain, maybe you can tell me what to do. I've tried everything . . . . prayer, A.A., self-control, yoga . . . . you name it. Nothing works. Alcohol is my god and my devil, my creator and my destroyer."

I would shake my head helplessly. Why should a lowly drug be able to destroy a man made in the image of God? It was beyond comprehension.

Ninety-eight percent of my pastoral counseling concerns family problems. The latest statistics put the divorce rate at a new high. In many marriages that do remain intact, sharp tensions exist.

Again and again people come to church and ask, "Pastor, what can I do about my wife? My husband? My children? Can you help me? Can you speak to them? Can you change them? I've tried so hard ... I've prayed, I've loved, I've done everything . . . nothing seems to work. Why is it that people can't love one another as they should? Why has God made us like this? Or does some alien power control our lives?"

What is that awful, fatal flaw that runs through human life? Why is it that man seems so bent upon self-destruction and so afraid of that one real source of help? Why are one million Americans going to die of lung cancer in the next five years because of cigaret smoking? Why do we destroy ourselves by wrong living, wrong eating, wrong thinking? We have found the enemy and he is *us*, as Stringfellow puts it.

Crime in the streets and in the White House .... white collar, blue collar, black and brown crime. Almost a dozen times in one year someone tried to break into the parsonage in the dead of night. People were mugged in front of the church and even in its own doorways.

My life was threatened several times, and one night death rang the doorbell disguised as the candy man. I was on the long-distance phone and didn't answer the doorbell. A man down the street died for me .... a black pastor, tied up, tortured and executed .... and all men's hearts, black and white, were filled with fear.

In Baltimore signs promote the occult on every college campus and even on many church doors. In Dundalk High School, Satan-worship cells actively recruit new members. In the many wooded areas of South Baltimore, students gather for drugs and sex and dark mysterious rites. At times I have received a dozen requests for deliverance in one week. Beautiful young girls reported invisible visitors in the night who left them covered with bruises and shame and nameless dread.

As if we didn't have enough of our own, we've imported demons from the East in record numbers. We used to send missionaries into Eastern heathen countries; now the stream is reversed, and the East is sending missionaries to us.

Several years ago I was skeptical about the reality of demons in our day. Fifteen years ago I considered the possibility of demon possession to be a sick medieval joke. But not any more. Again and again, before the altar of the Lord, at the sacred name of Jesus, something has departed. Sometimes shrieks and unholy laughter and violent illness left the victim limp and torn.

The crises that threaten the world also exist in the Church. Torn by strife and dissension, the Body of Christ is threatened by secularism, irrelevance and indifference. Every single day thousands of members abandon the Church. The Roman Catholic church is running out of priests, and parts of my church seem to be programmed for self-destruct. The Gospel is moving away from the Reformation lands toward the Third World.

Money obviously is not the answer. All our money has not been able to buy us friends or security or to solve our social and moral problems. While bringing benefits, technology and knowledge have also improved our methods of destruction and created new problems.

Medicine and science are not the answer . . . . the better medicine becomes, the more people seem to get sick. If you don't believe it, try to find a parking space near a modern hospital. Medicine and science have promised much: elimination of disease, poverty and even the eventual defeat of death itself. The promise is yet unfulfilled, but they *have* succeeded in extending the time, pain and expense of dying.

The great social and economic programs of the sixties failed to eliminate poverty or bring about equality and justice. The cores of many of our great cities have become ghettos, unsanitary and abandoned by the Church. The city schools are in shambles, with the average seventh-grader performing four years below his grade level. The S.A.T. scores of our students are going down each year. As classes become larger and discipline becomes more lax, the goal of the teacher is to get through one more day alive. The pupil's goal is to sleep, play and get free food.

As America observes its bicentennial, can it take a real inventory of itself? What has gone wrong and what is the answer? The easy and the hard answers haven't worked. Have we perhaps been asking the wrong questions or overlooking something simple and obvious? Is it time perhaps to try God's answers, or do we need another two hundred years of blood and toil and tears?

Will another century of burning and breaking and hurting and hating bring us to our knees and to God's throne of grace? Is it too soon or too late? Can intercession, deep sacrificial intercession, still save us?

2

THE DOCTRINE OF MAN

Jesus, we thank You that You share everything with us. Every knife cuts You, every pain is Your pain, every cancer is Yours, too. We praise You that You are not only on the mountain tops but also in the bottom of the valleys. In the dark night of the soul when we think that God has abandoned us, reach out with that nail-pierced hand and touch us.

God, don't waste our pain. Let no tear fall unseen, no cry be unheard, no sigh in the night go unnoticed. Take every burden and every sigh, every prayer and every cry and place them on Your whip-scarred back. The cross means that You totally share all our woe. Help us to believe that You understand and care about everything. Teach us always to praise, no matter how dark things may seem at the moment.

Father, we thank You for the Word, "that the sufferings of this present time are not worth comparing with the glory that shall be revealed in us." When we cry out in anguish and doubt to the Father, undergird our prayers by Your total sharing.

In the cross of Jesus, amen.

How did we get into this mess anyhow? We cannot blame Satan entirely. He is indeed the head of a vast and personal conspiracy of evil, but he also gets blamed for a lot of things he doesn't do. Can we blame the fall of man or the will of God for everything that has gone wrong?

Certainly some of the blame lies in the wrong doctrine of man. What is man anyhow? What is he for? What is the meaning and the goal of human existence? There is no doubt that science, philosophy and even the church have gone astray because of wrong doctrines of man. Our misconceptions have kept us from praying effectively.

If you try to repair a washing machine with the wiring diagram from your lawnmower, chaos, confusion and destruction are sure to follow. You can't raise Siberian huskies as if they were goldfish or canaries. In order to be able to deal with something, it is basic that you know first of all what it is and what it is for.

The secular doctrines of man assume at least that he is a thinking, tool-using animal. According to the doctrine of evolution, he came from nature via the sea. When his brief span of life is over, he will return to nature via the dust and stay there. The function of his existence is to be born, to play and to work, to eat and to sleep, to laugh and to cry, to create, procreate, and then to die. The supreme goals in life are security, success, pleasure and the avoidance of pain. Or as the Bill of Rights says, "Life, Liberty and the Pursuit of Happiness."

The Church too has often operated with a false doctrine of man, assuming a dichotomy or split between matter and spirit. According to this dualism, body and soul, matter and spirit, time and eternity, sacred and secular, are separate things that seldom touch or interact.

Thomas Aquinas, the great medieval theologian of the church, believed that nature and grace exist together but seldom meet. This kind of split makes the Church withdraw from human problems and become irrelevant and indifferent to the social context. The believer simply gets saved, sanctified, and shines the church bench with the seat of his pants while he piously waits for "pie in the sky by and by."

Another erroneous religious view of man is sometimes called "humanism." The church does indeed try to relate in a meaningful way to human needs and problems. By doing so, it sometimes forgets the vertical dimension; that is, that the power to relate to human life in a healing way can come from God alone.

In the inner city and in the chaplaincy, we have tried very hard to become relevant, but it seems that every time we become secularized because we give up our God language. The difficulty is in maintaining a balance between the vertical-horizontal dimensions.

The cross has two beams, one points upward and the other points outward. The upward beam represents our relationship to God and His to us. It points up to heaven and down to earth. It is the Jacob's ladder on which the angels ascend and descend carrying up our prayers and praise and bringing down God's forgiveness, salvation, His Spirit, and all His blessings.

At the same time the horizontal bars point out to all the world. That horizontal beam is like the arms of God that embrace the whole creation. They show that His love from heaven, offered to the earth from the cross, embraces all men and all human need. The Church has a unique function in the world. When it forgets its uniqueness or fails to claim its wholeness, the salt has lost its savor.

Jesus came into the world to heal the whole man—body, soul and spirit—for time and eternity. Before He left the world He gave His disciples "the great commission," to bring the whole word to the whole man in the whole world. The God who sees the sparrow's fall and counts the hairs of our head is concerned about every area of our existence. In the wholeness of God's salvation, the lines between sacred and secular, spirit and matter, blur. Sunday and Monday, worship and work, flow together in that eternal wholeness God came to give.

The model for God's working in the world is the Incarnation. When matter and spirit come together, the frontiers tend to become blurred and disappear. Anyone meeting the Jesus of history would have confronted at one and the same time the eternal Spirit and the authentic man. Yet, there was and is no way for us to define accurately the interaction between these completely opposite entities. For instance, we could not say that Jesus was man from the waist on down and God from the waist up, or that he was man until twelve noon and God the rest of the time. We simply have to accept this wonderful mystery that somehow in one real human being the eternal Father was fully present.

Perhaps the Apostle John understood it better than anyone else. He tries to describe his own perception of the Incarnation in the opening verses of his first epistle. He says, "This word which we have heard and seen and touched with our hands, this word of life, is what we want to impart to you." (Many of the Scripture verses used in this book are the author's free translations.)

30

Again, in his Gospel in the first chapter he tries to explain the mystery. "In the beginning was the Word, and the Word was with God, and the Word was God." The Word, the *Logos*, which means the ultimate and infinite principle of reality, "was made flesh and dwelt among us and we beheld His glory, the glory of the only begotten Son, full of grace and truth."

Sometimes I imagine that John must have reached these conclusions in the following manner. He had seen the wedding at Cana, the feeding of the five thousand, the stilling of the storm and the healing of the sick. The man who did these great miracles was his best friend and his daily companion. According to outward appearances, he was like other men. He'd get hungry and tired, sweaty and dirty. He ate and drank and walked and slept like all other men. He was made of flesh and blood, bones, hair and skin, like other men.

Perhaps one night, as they were sleeping under the clear desert skies of Palestine, with the stars so bright they seemed near enough to touch, John alone remained awake. He began to think. He began to ask himself deep theological and philosophical questions. Who was this man, really? Was his best friend and daily companion, this man sleeping next to him, really the same as the eternal, infinite Spirit? Was Jesus really a man at all?

Perhaps then, carefully and quietly, in the mysterious desert silence he reached out and touched Jesus. He touched His beard, he felt the dust, the sweat on His skin; in the fire light John saw the brown of His body caused by the burning desert sun. He felt the firm flesh and the hard muscles of His arms and shoulders. He heard the breathing, perhaps even the snoring, of his Master. He saw His chest move up and down, he heard His heart beat and even felt His pulse.

Yes, He was real, really real, an authentic man, and

yet, somehow, in some incredible way, also the eternal Word, the creator and preserver of all things. This is the ultimate mystery that beats at our clay-shuttered doors.

The Incarnation helps us understand all interaction between flesh and spirit, time and eternity, matter and nonmatter. We see this in the Church, first of all. The Church is both human and divine.

We know that the Church is human because we belong to it. "If you find the perfect church, don't join it—you'll ruin it." Yet, if we didn't believe that the Church was divine, we would have no part of it.

The same is true of the Bible. We believe it is both human and divine. It's the written Word of God, born in the cradle of human history. It was written by men under the inspiration of the Holy Spirit.

When we try to separate the human and the divine, we become involved in destructive and useless controversies. The fundamentalist fails to see the human dimension, and the liberal fails to see the divine. Both miss the point. For, here in one book we have the mingling of matter and spirit, of human and divine.

The same principle is true of ourselves. We are both matter and spirit. Yet, when we try to separate our flesh and our spirit, we become involved in the mystery of human motivation. Our motives are always mixed, always more complex and worse than we think they are. We are fallen human beings in whom the Spirit of the eternal God dwells, in some mysterious interaction with our spirits.

Man was made for one reason only, for fellowship with God. In order to have this fellowship with God, he must contain the divine life of the Trinity. We were not meant to live merely by the power of our biological life, but through Christ in us. Man is a kind of being or a kind of machine that is wired for AC and DC. This

32

means, if he is born again, he is able to plug into the AC of God and live directly from the life of God's Spirit. This is what Paul means when he says in Galatians 2:20, "Henceforth, it is no longer I that live, but Christ who lives in me."

But man can also live by DC, that is, through his biological batteries. These batteries, however, run down and die and their energy is finite. To walk in the Spirit means to live in this present life plugged into the eternal life of God. To walk in the flesh, according to the law of sin and death, means to live from our natural biological batteries until they run down.

Bodies separate, but spirits unite. No matter how close two human beings may be to each other, they are separated from each other by their bodies, their personalities. Words were intended to communicate and to reveal, but they often conceal more than they reveal. Words do not always unite, but often separate people. On the other hand, spirits unite and interpenetrate.

The Spirit of God comes to our spirit and fuses with it, so that God is closer to us than our own thoughts. He is more real to us than our own hands and feet. God wants to live out His entire life in us, not only the spiritual life. He wants to beat in our hearts, think in our minds, breathe in our lungs, and flow in our blood and walk with our feet. He wants to be in every atom and electron of our bodies.

Since the Incarnation, God does nothing in the world except through means. Christ has no hands and feet, no voice except ours. He has no instruments or channels, except ours, because we are His body. The principle of God's total life now indwelling us has some very practical implications. It also taught me some new truths about intercession.

In June of 1974 I attended an international conference in Seattle, Washington. One morning at breakfast, a Methodist minister and I began to talk about healing.

"Pastor Prange," he began, "I have heard you mention healing a number of times at this conference. I wonder if you might be able to help me."

"Well, *I* can't help you but perhaps God can. What is your problem?" I asked routinely.

"I was a bombardier in World War II and my eardrums were destroyed in a tremendous explosion. Now I am a minister of the Methodist church and have three congregations to take care of. My hearing is getting worse and worse. I can hear only a little, mostly by lip reading. The doctors tell me that my eardrums are gone, and that the area is completely grown over with scar tissue."

We went into the little chapel before the morning meeting. Silently I prayed, *Lord, give me the right prayer to pray for this man.* And suddenly the words came, silently but clearly and plainly: *It is impossible for Pastor Estes to hear with his physical ears, but he is filled with the life of Christ. Pray that from now on he will hear with the ears of Christ.*

I thought, *the physical ears of Christ? Wasn't His life in us just spiritual and eternal?*

Then the gift of directed prayer came—straight from the will of God. I heard myself praying, "Lord, I pray that my brother may henceforth hear with the ears of Christ. Christ's eardrums are not broken or covered with scar tissue. Let the divine life that lives in Brother Estes be complete, and let it take over the gaps and the tasks of his physical, emotional and natural life."

From that moment on Pastor Estes was able to hear perfectly, even though his ears did not change. The doctors still tell him that it is impossible for him to hear with the ears he has and he always agrees. In a recent letter he said, "At the Spokane conference in 1975, a grandma who had nerve deafness heard me sharing how the Lord had healed my ears. She asked and, *praise Him*, she was healed, too! He is wonderful!"

In Seattle I prayed that same prayer with four other pastors but it didn't work. It wasn't God's prayer for them. But it was God's prayer and His will for the lady that Pastor Estes wrote me about.

God is a Trinity and man is a trinity. Man is a trinity consisting of body, soul and spirit. The body is the outer man; the soul, the inner man; and the spirit, the innermost man. Like the divine Trinity, the human trinity forms a perfect unity in the personality. This is in sharp contrast to the Greek division of body and soul. It also conflicts with the dualism of matter and spirit so often found in human philosophies and religions. In the Hebrew doctrine of man, each part has a distinct function which interacts with the whole. There are some fifteen hundred passages in the Bible which deal with body and soul and spirit.

Man's body is his material outer garment. It relates to the natural environment through his senses. The biological, the chemical make-up of the human body, form a continuous link with all of life. We share cells and protoplasm with all living things. We also share atoms and electrons with organic matter. Even our blood is mostly sea water.

At death, the physical body falls off like a worn-out garment and returns to the dust from which it came (Ecclesiastes 12:7). The body is not the self. When its purpose is completed, it is put aside. The body, or the flesh, is man's material self and is never converted. It is like the outer court of the Temple whose usefulness is temporary and limited.

The "soul" in the Bible, means primarily the "self." It serves as the buffer zone between matter and spirit. It is also the animating principle of the physical body. That means, man is not a body which contains a soul, but he is a soul which wears a body. In its natural aspect, the soul is mortal but as self, it carries the identity beyond death.

Soul is greater than body as spirit is greater than soul. Here are all the vast powers and creative potential of man. The soul is so powerful it often usurps and counterfeits the functions of the spirit.

The three primary functions of the soul are: mind, emotion and will. The baffling medical-psychological mind-body problem is perhaps hidden in the mystery of the soul. That is to say, that neither medicine, psychology nor philosophy know exactly how the mind and the body interact. This interaction of the physical, material and the nonmaterial self, takes place in the buffer zone of the soul.

Man has a spirit and God is a Spirit. The two are not the same although the Bible does not always distinguish between them in a precise fashion. The spirit of man is the only part of man to which God comes directly. It is man's innermost self, his Holy of Holies. Spirit is deeper than soul. Its functions are conscience, intuition and communion.

Conscience, in this connection, means knowledge of God's will which is not culturally or intellectually acquired.

Intuition is knowing God's will in the same way that God knows; that is, without direct access to sources of information.

Communion is the unique human ability to relate directly to, and to commune with, the Infinite Creator's Spirit.

Man is unique in function and purpose, in that his spirit is able to have direct access to the Infinite Spirit of God. In Romans 8:11, Paul says that "If the Spirit of Him who raised Jesus Christ from the dead is in you, then He will give life to your mortal bodies through the same Spirit which dwells in you."

If the eternal Spirit lives in us, then He not only gives us faith and eternal life, but He quickens, He gives wholeness and power and health to this mortal frame as well. In the depths of the human spirit the divine and human identities seem to fuse as the Holy Spirit prays for us and with us and through us.

The practical implications of this Biblical doctrine of man are tremendous. There are applications that cover almost every field of human endeavor. Through God's Spirit, our spirits, which were thrown out of the driver's seat by the fall into sin, can again take over the authority in our souls and bodies.

In the temptation of Jesus to turn stones into bread we see that spirit was intended to rule body. "Man shall not live by bread alone." In other words, the spirit of man was intended to be a captain of the ship of his life. We were not intended to be the victims of our bodies and emotions, but the masters of them.

Emotional, physical, and other kinds of healing can take place when the human spirit, again through the power of God's Spirit, resumes command of the total person. Deep healing, healing of the memories, release from worry, phobias and other oppressions, can take place when we become fully aware of the function and power of the reborn human spirit.

Many times this approach can be used in counseling. For example, a man came to me who was a very spiritual man but was entirely unable to stop smoking. We discussed the Biblical doctrine of man and the fact that Christ's Spirit and his spirit could take authority over the drives in the body and the soul. We prayed that the Infinite Spirit of Christ in him might, through his spirit, command the soul to transmit the message to the entire body that from henceforth there would be a negative reaction to smoking. We prayed that the very smell of cigaret smoke might make him ill, and that he might lose completely his desire for tobacco, physiologically and psychologically.

On the way home from our session he was deep in thought and somehow forgot what we had prayed. As he was driving his car, he automatically reached for a cigaret. When he placed it into his mouth, it tasted so terrible that he gagged. Suddenly he became nauseous, and from that time on he has not been able to smoke or to be close to people who do.

In another case, a young man—also very spiritual, and deeply afflicted with allergies, especially hay fever—came to me. Most of the time he had difficulty in breathing. His eyes were red. We talked about this principle of the doctrine of man at some length. Finally we began to pray.

"Lord," I prayed, "You have made Your son in Your image to rule the physical creation in Your place. You have also, in the new birth, through the resurrection of Jesus, given him Your image. You have filled him with the gifts of Your Spirit. Now show him that the double image of God, plus the special ministry of Your Spirit, can assume control over his entire personality.

"You have made him and the creation to be in harmony with each other. You have made him to be the lord over Your creation. Therefore, through Your power and covenant, let his spirit command the histamines and the hormones of his body to react in an obedient and harmonious way with all of Your creation. As You have made him to be lord over the physical and the spiritual creation, so let him now be lord and master over his body and soul through Your Spirit. Amen."

Almost instantly the symptoms of his allergy began to fade. After a few weeks, he had total relief. There had been regressions, but each time when he reclaims the authority of God's Spirit and his own spirit over his entire body and person, the symptoms retreat.

This *doctrine of man*, if properly understood and used, can destroy phobias, heal memories, and enable one to control fantasies, as well. Sometimes I pray with people who say, "Pastor, I simply can't help myself. I can't control my thoughts and fantasies. I don't seem to have any power at all over my feelings. I know I ought to praise the Lord and rejoice. I know that I ought to trust and not to fear, but somehow I cannot. I'm afraid. I feel anxiety and sometimes terror, even though I keep telling myself that the Lord is near. What can I do?"

In cases like this, we often pray something like the following: "Lord, we pray for the healing of the memories. Bring all the past and all the hidden wounds of this person into that eternal moment before You. Let everything be brought into the light of Your presence. Release emotions and the soul from all bitterness and distortion and flood them with the love of Christ.

"Conform this will to Your will—joyfully, freely and fully. Through the soul, let all the cells of the body be commanded to perform their tasks harmoniously and efficiently, according to Your perfect plan. If there are rebellious, uncontrolled emotions, thoughts or fantasies present, rebuke them.

"Command the storm inside this personality to be still. If there are immature cancer cells present or disobedient incomplete hormones, let them be commanded to obey the unity of this body, which You envisioned and planned before the creation of the world. Whatever is sick . . . . heal; whatever is weak . . . . strengthen; whatever is missing . . . . replace. That which is alien and hurtful, bind and drive out.

"Let the life of Christ, with all its power, joy, love, light and beauty, flow through every cell, atom, hormone and electron of his body. Let every cell and every

39

electron together praise the Lord! Say, Hallelujah! Rejoice in His life and His light and His presence, and obey His perfect will and plan. Amen."

The risen life of Christ is, through the Spirit, a reality which covers both sides of the grave. We have gained far more in Christ than Adam lost. Adam and Eve had not yet eaten of the Tree of Life when they were expelled from Paradise. But we, through Jesus Christ and through the gift of His Spirit, have received and eaten of that water and that bread of life. Therefore, the reborn human spirit is the only place in all of creation where the uncreated life of God may be found. Not even the archangels have it. They are creatures but we are sons by adoption.

When we call God Father, it is the Spirit Himself bearing witness with our spirit, that we are children of God, and, if children, then heirs, heirs of God and fellow heirs with Christ (Romans 8:15-17). God, the center of all personality, comes to the center of our personality and says "Yes" to Himself inside of us. This "Abba Father," "Yes, Daddy," is the assurance that we are sons by adoption.

Galatians 5:16-26 talks about walking in the Spirit and walking in the flesh. This means that the reborn Christian has a choice of two totally different dimensions or life styles. If he walks only in the flesh, he is subject to all the laws of sin and death. This means that he operates according to the principle of natural life in every way, and is subject to all the limitations of a fallen world. The law of sin and death is not evil in itself. It comes from God and gives order and stability to the natural creation, but it cannot give us the life of God.

On the other hand, as Romans 8 spells out, the reborn believer can walk in the Spirit. In the dimension of the Spirit all things are possible, because the Spirit is the foretaste or the down payment of the life to come. This means that the Holy Spirit is the carrier of eternal life. The New Testament Greek word which has been translated as, "down payment or earnest money," in English usage, means something that we give or pay for, as a hold on some future possession.

In the New Testament, God through the Spirit gives us the down payment or the earnest money of the inheritance to come. In the dimension of divine healing, deliverance, conversion and miracles, the supernatural and the abnormal are normal. The laws of cause and effect and of scientific determinism are not suspended, but are simply superseded by the higher law of the Spirit.

Behaviorism in psychology is based upon the principle that everything is part of a long chain of cause and effect. In the law of the Spirit, this is not true. The Spirit is parachuted in directly from above. He is not related or bound by previous conditions or causes. This is a gift that comes directly from God.

The Spirit brings us the quality and the quantity of life which God Himself lives and is. Eternal life begins here for those who walk according to the Spirit and not in the flesh. Through the Spirit God's salvation reaches into every area of this present life with its healing and transforming power.

As Christians, we live in two worlds simultaneously; that is, as people who live the life of Christ but are still a part of this fallen world and still wear fallen bodies. This causes frustration, failure and the conflict that the Apostle Paul described when he said, "For the good that I wish, I do not do; but I practice the very evil that I do not wish" (Romans 7:19).

Before we can truly walk in the Spirit, both body and soul have to be broken. This is a painful process because it means dying. As we die and rise with Christ each day, the new man is being formed within us.

In the depths and in the dying, the second Adam, the Man from Heaven, breaks through and becomes real and is actualized already in this present world. When the history of Jesus Christ becomes our own history, we can walk with Him in the dimension of Spirit, and receive everything directly from God's hand.

Jesus' temptation in the wilderness was a temptation of body, soul and spirit. In the first temptation, the enemy tried to get Him to use His divine power to satisfy the hunger of His body. The second temptation was directed to the soul. It was an appeal to the pride and ambition of man. "I will give you all the kingdoms of the world, if you will fall down and worship Me."

The third temptation was of the spirit. "Jump down from the temple." In other words win men by being a miracle worker rather than by suffering. In every temptation the theology of glory was pitted against the theology of the cross.

Jesus was triumphant in every case. He set the pattern and established God's priorities for us. Man is made to live the life and do the will of God. We are to glorify God and enjoy Him forever. There is a God-shaped vacuum inside of us that only God can fill. Every hunger is finally a God-hunger. He has made us for Himself and we cannot rest until we rest in Him. Every life is an extension and manifestation of the one Life, and every love a dim and far off echo of that eternal love that beckons from the cross.

3

THE PROBLEM OF PAIN

Lord, give Your power to the medicine, Your skill to the doctor, Your love and anointing to all who minister to Your sick ones. As You once healed all who came to You in the days of Your flesh, continue to heal now through Your Word and Church.

Jesus, Great Physician, Healer of men's souls and bodies, do what medicine and science cannot do: heal the whole person. Let the Father's will on earth be done through whole and holy channels as it is in heaven. As our days, so may our strength be. Until our work is done and You call us home, may we be strong and effective channels of Your love.

Father, Your glory is man, fully alive, so fill the temples of our bodies with the beauty of praise and the incense of thanksgiving. Make us living prayers, forever offering up our lives for Your glory. May we be changed into Your likeness from glory unto glory and we praise You.

Jesus, You bore our sicknesses on Your body; by Your stripes we have been healed. Show us that we do not have to bear them alone or in vain. Let Your stripes heal all our diseases.

In the name of Him
Who came to lay His wounds
on all the wounds of the world.

The most frequently asked question in the world is: "If God is good then why is there so much pain in the world?" or "Why do bad things happen to good people and especially to me?" There is enough pain in one alley of one big city ghetto or in the terminal cancer ward of one hospital to convince even the greatest unbelieving optimist that God isn't good.

What about the silence of God over the cruel and ugly tragedy of human history? How could a loving God be indifferent to the slaughters of this century? Does He have nothing to say about the incredible suffering of the prisoners in the German, the Russian and the Chinese death camps?

These mass tragedies somehow seem to pass us by and leave us untouched as long as they happen to someone else. It is only when pain and tragedy become personal, when it strikes close to home, that we cry out. And then we cry the cry of Job, "Why God? Why? Why me? What did I do? Am I any worse than anyone else? For what am I being punished?"

Sometimes when we look at the vast bloody human drama, we want to have a confrontation with God. If He would just speak one clear ringing word and tell us what it all means! "If He would just rend the heavens and come down, that the mountains might quake in His presence" (Isaiah 64). If we truly understand the problem of pain and the answers to these questions, we are ready for effective intercession.

It's easy to blame God for everything that happens, since He is all-powerful. Some passages in the Old Testament back up this feeling. Isaiah 45:6, 7 says: "I am the Lord . . . causing well-being and creating calamity; I am the Lord who does all these."

Perhaps the clearest expression of God's involvement in good and evil is to be found in Deuteronomy 28. This is the great Old Testament chapter about the blessings and the cursings. This puts good and evil in a simple cause-and-effect relationship that we can understand. The book of Job points toward a more complex relationship. God permits but He does not cause. Satan, himself, is used by God for a higher purpose.

The New Testament makes it abundantly clear that in the "new covenant" sickness and evil do not come from God. Jesus came into the world to free us from the bondage of pain and evil. He came to heal the whole man—body and soul and spirit—for time and eternity. He came to destroy the works of the devil, to lay His wounded hands upon all the wounds and pain and the sin of the world.

In Acts 10:38 His ministry is summed up, "He went about doing good, healing all that were oppressed by the devil." In the synagogue in Nazareth He quoted Isaiah 61:1-3 to introduce His ministry. He read, "The Spirit of the Lord is upon Me; He has anointed Me to make the blind to see, to free the captives, to preach good news to the poor."

Again, Jesus summed up the meaning of His ministry to the disciples and John the Baptist. They came to ask Him: "Are You really the one who is to come or do we look for another?"

His answer was, "Go and tell John what you see and hear." He didn't say, "Go ask the priests or the Pharisees," or "Go look it up in your theology books." Rather, He said, "Look around you, see what's happening: the blind are receiving their sight and the lame are walking, lepers are being cleansed, the deaf hear and the dead are being raised and the poor have the Gospel preached to them" (Matthew 11:3-5).

Each time He is challenged on the validity and the authority of His Messianic office, Jesus identifies Himself with healing and deliverance—release from the captivity of evil. If God was the one who caused the pain and the evil, then the ministry and the Messianic identity of Jesus would make no sense.

Evil, pain and sin are not the perfect will of God. In Luke 13:16 Jesus refers to a sick woman as the daughter of Abraham whom Satan had bound for eighteen years. James 1:17 says that God is the Father of lights from whom every good and perfect gift comes. In verse 13 of chapter 1, James warns that no man should say when he is tempted that he is tempted by God, because God cannot tempt men with evil. In Matthew 7:9-11, the evangelist says that God is the kind of father who cannot give bad gifts to His children. He does not give stones for bread or serpents instead of fish. God is a good father and He cannot give a bad gift.

Pain and tragedy are not a direct punishment for sin. In John 9 Jesus says of the man born blind, "It was not that this man sinned, or his parents, but that the works of God might be manifested in him" (John 9:3). In Luke 13 Jesus points out that those on whom the tower of Siloam fell, as well as the Galileans whose blood Pilate mingled with their sacrifices, were no worse sinners than anyone else (Luke 13:1-5). We are all guilty and the harvest of sin is reaped indiscriminately by a fallen world. Sin is the cause of sickness and death but not necessarily on a one-to-one basis.

It is easy to fall into some kind of dualism and believe that there is a self-existent power of evil that is independent of God's creation. But that would not be Biblical. Satan is powerful; he is the mortal enemy of God and man, but he was created by God. This is clearly brought out by both Isaiah and Ezekiel (Isaiah 14 and Ezekiel 28). Satan fell down from heaven (Luke 10:17-19). We are dealing with a defeated enemy. All that is left are pockets of resistance and certain mopping-up operations.

Evil has only the power that God allows, and it has only the time that God is allotting. In God's children, Satan has only the power and the freedom that we personally grant him. In a world where man is free and in rebellion and where an invisible conspiracy of evil still exists, what ought one to expect? When God makes creatures who are both powerful and free, He makes Himself a little less free. The cross shows us that somehow love and pain go together. The price for sin is God's total self-giving.

But who, then, is responsible for all the pain and evil and tragedy in the world? If God does not will it, if Satan has been defeated, and if man tries to escape it, where does it all come from? As we have seen before, man himself is perhaps the author of 75 percent of all his pain. Most untimely deaths come from man's abuse of his own freedom.

War, automobile accidents, tobacco, alcohol, drugs, wrong eating and wrong living, as well as wrong thinking, are the primary causes for the problem of pain. Man then is the principal author of his own pain and tragedy. But because no man is an island unto himself; the sin, the carelessness and the guilt of others often affect the innocent.

Pain and evil come from man and Satan who were both created by God. Evil is not the sovereign will of God but a necessary condition of the gift of freedom. In the kind of world where faith, freedom and love can exist, evil and rebellion are inescapable.

All these answers somehow fall short. How does an Almighty, an all-compassionate God, relate to the problem of pain without becoming at least guilty of indifference or the sin of omission? If He does not send pain, does He then permit and use it for a higher purpose? This is by far the most tempting answer to the problem of pain. It is a partial answer, but does not cover the entire question.

The epistle to the Hebrews says, "My son, do not regard lightly the discipline of the Lord, nor faint when you are reproved by Him. For those whom the Lord loves He disciplines, and He scourges every son whom He receives" (Hebrews 12:5-6). Verses 7 through 11 of the same chapter go on to say that we are disciplined because we are sons, in order that we might yield the fruits of righteousness. This is certainly true of limited personal pain. For every prayer that rises in prosperity, a thousand rise in adversity.

Is not God in the depths and on the margins of life? Does He not have to get our attention before we will turn toward Him and seek His face? And yet, just how are we disciplined and chastened or made to grow by the death camps and the mass graves of war? How do the horrible natural catastrophes that bring incredible destruction upon the earth discipline anyone?

My personal pain can lead me to God but the death of millions in war only makes me question the goodness of God. When the unbeliever sees the total picture of evil, it becomes very difficult for him to believe in a God of love.

Pain and the Will of God

The prayer of Gethsemane, "Thy will be done," is not an answer. At the very best, it is a kind of pious fatal-

48

ism or dull resignation. At worst, it is unbelief or even blasphemy. It could be that we are saying, "God, I don't really believe that you answer prayer or that you still heal, so this lets us both off the hook."

There is no example in the New Testament of Jesus or the disciples using this prayer in connection with a healing. If sickness is God's will, we should neither pray nor take medicine. If He sent it, why should we ask Him to take it away? If pain is really the will of God, then even taking an aspirin to relieve a headache would be going against His will and plan.

It's so easy simply to shrug one's shoulders and say, "What can I do? God, You are all-powerful. Who can go against Your will?" Passive resignation is not faith. Faith is trust and love in action.

Sometimes when tragedy strikes, pious people bow their heads grimly and mutter through clenched teeth, "It was the will of God." How do they say it—joyfully or bitterly? Is God's will the tragic and the painful, and our will the good and the sweet? Or is it perhaps the other way around?

When a plane crashes and kills a hundred people because a bomb was planted on it, the bomber is called a mad monster. But when a plane crashes because of lightning and kills a hundred people, it is called "an act of God." If someone sneaked into a nursery and planted typhoid germs in a baby's body, he would be a super-criminal. Yet, how often do we bow our heads when a baby dies and say unctuously, "the will of God"? It was God's will, so we simply share pagan fatalism.

What if it was not God's will at all? Is He some depraved monster who goes about crashing planes and killing babies, or is He a loving heavenly Father who counts the hairs of our head and watches the sparrows fall? Is He the Father of lights from whom every good and perfect gift comes, or is He the grim author of human tragedy? Can He possibly be both at the same time? Can we love and trust the cause of all pain or do we simply fear Him?

Jesus taught us to pray, "Thy will be done on earth as it is in heaven." In heaven the will of God is done through perfect instruments, spiritually, morally, totally. There is no cancer, no pain, no typhoid in heaven.

In the same way God wants His will to be done on earth through perfect instruments. He cannot play on a broken violin. He does not want to be glorified in a shattered and ruined temple. God is more glorified in our healing than in our sicknesses. He *never* looks at a cancer or polio victim or someone crippled by cerebral palsy or arthritis and says, "This is how I planned you before the foundations of the world were laid." He always says, as He said to the leper, "I will; be thou clean."

Intercession is God's channel to do His will in the world. Since the incarnation, God goes through channels. The Spirit is not a ghost but a Divine Person looking for bodies to be God's temple and do His will. Christ has no body in the world today except His Church. We are His only hands and feet.

The intercessor is the medicine and the scalpel for the one great Physician who alone can heal. The intercessor on his knees is the channel for God's healing love to a broken world. We are not mere spectators at the drama of creation, redemption and healing, but partners with God through intercession.

God is always on the side of healing under conditions, some of which we know and most of which we do not, some of which we can fulfill and many of which we cannot. He does not enjoy pain for pain's sake. He does not will unnecessary suffering because He has to share it with us. He has a different perspective and a different set of priorities than we do.

God's Relationship to Pain and Evil

God's relationship to the problem of pain is terribly complex. It is perhaps best summed up in Acts 2:23, "This Jesus, delivered up according to the deliberate plan and foreknowledge of God, you crucified and killed through the hands of lawless men." There is a divine plan, there are human agents, and there is human guilt.

In the case of Judas, Satan also enters the picture. Judas in his freedom was tempted. Judas wanted to make a "fast buck" or had some higher, mixed motivation. When he sought an opportunity to betray Jesus, Satan got into the act. Once Judas had sought the opportunity to betray Jesus and Satan had entered his heart, then God became involved in order that the Scriptures might be fulfilled.

God, somehow and somewhere, writes the script. He even describes the characters, the players, in the eternal drama. Satan enters in and tries to use the elements of freedom, of sin and rebellion, to defeat both God and man. Yet, the characters in the drama somehow choose their own roles.

In one sense each man chooses, within the context of God's calling, to be a Judas or a Peter or a John. The Gospel is happening now. Jesus is still suffering, Judas still betraying, and Peter still denying. Pilate and Caiaphas sit in perpetual judgment. What part do you play?

Romans 8:28 gives us the final key to the problem of pain. It says that God works in everything for good with those who love Him and are called according to

51

His own purpose. God's love is a forgiving, a redeeming, and a calling love. His relationship to evil and pain is neither permissive nor willing, but redemptive.

He is able and willing to "trump the devil's ace" and turn the whole conspiracy into good. The power of His calling love can transform all things, good or evil, into eternal glory. To make good things, men need good material. God can create with any kind of material, good or bad. He can even use sin as His worker and evil as His bricks.

God redeems pain by sharing it. On the cross He forever identified Himself with all human sin and tragedy. Every pain is His pain, every cancer is His cancer, every knife cuts Him too. He who counts the hairs of our head and sees the sparrow's fall, somehow feels with us all our pain.

So often when people come to me with a deep tragedy, they ask the question, "Does God know about this, does He understand?"

I usually say, "I'm sure that He not only knows and understands, but He also feels this with you because nothing that happens can be outside of His all-knowing love and concern."

When you reach out in the darkness, you will find an invisible hand; if you press it hard enough, you can feel the nail hole in it. When we cry out in despair, "My God, my God, why hast thou forsaken me?" there is an answering echo in the darkness. The important thing is when we cry out that we always say with Jesus, "My God, my God," never just, "God."

When we ask, "Why does God let this happen? Why is God so unjust?" that could be blasphemy. But when we say with Jesus on the cross, "My God," that's a prayer, a deep and desperate prayer. That's a cry that God cannot refuse to hear.

Manfried Houseman has described the picture, "The

Christ of Sigmeringen," under the title, "One Must Watch." The picture shows Jesus in Gethsemane. John is quietly sleeping on his breast; Peter and James are sleeping some distance away. Tension, anxiety, the implications of the moment, are simply too much for human emotions. All their fuses are burned out; they have simply gone to sleep.

Jesus asked them, "Could you not watch with Me for one hour?" Yet, He knew the answer. For what was happening here was far, far too deep and too heavy for one who is only mortal. In the picture one sees incredible agony and yet eternal peace in Christ's face.

His eyes seem to search out over all the world. He sees every battlefield and every hospital and sick room. His all-seeing eye knows every secret sin and reads every guilty conscience. All the cries, all the moans and the groans of the total human tragedy—past, present and future—ring in His ears.

He knows every evil, twisted thought and heart. Every sin becomes His sin and every pain His, too. The burden is too much for even a God-man. His Spirit is deeply distressed. His sweat comes down as great drops of blood. His fear is that somehow in this terrible hour His human will may be separated from the Father's. He cries out, "Nevertheless, not My will but Thine be done." Then the angels come and strengthen Him to drink the bitter cup to the dregs.

He is still drinking that cup and somehow we share it with Him. Every pain and need we turn over to Him becomes a part of the Father's redemptive will. The cup is no longer bitter but sweet because it comes from the hand of the Father. We receive all things, not from fate or the enemy or our own fallen wills, but as a perfect gift from the Father's love. In this light, the only possible response to pain is praise. "Count it all joy," the Apostle Peter says (1 Peter 3:6-9).

Romans 8:18-25 suggests the highest answer to the

problem of pain. Man is fallen and the creation has fallen with him. Man will be redeemed and so will the creation. The signal is to be the redemption of our bodies. In the meantime we groan under the bondage to corruption and decay. But we groan in hope. This is a hope for something which we have never experienced and cannot even imagine. The glorious fulfillment of this hope will make the sufferings of this present time unworthy to be considered.

Long before the galaxies were formed they existed in the thought of God; all beauty, love and joy were already there in His mind. But pain and tragedy were there, too, since nothing can escape the all-seeing eye of God's consciousness.

On that first dewy morning of creation, God already heard the flies buzzing around the cross. He already felt the nails in the hands and feet of His beloved Son. In that moment of perfect creation before a man was created, God already felt the weight of mankind's sin pressing down upon the cross. In the choking thirst and the thick darkness of Calvary, the pain of creation was already focusing. The angels and the morning stars sang together even as the moans and groans began to echo in the dim and distant future.

If God knew all of this, why did He go through with it? Is the prize really worth the price? What if man had not fallen? He might have remained an eternal, innocent infant in God's heavenly nursery, scarcely conscious of all the glory and love surrounding him. Because of what God and man have suffered together, God is able to prepare a destiny for us which is a hundred thousand times greater.

We can grow up to the stature and image of Jesus Christ and become "Sons of God by adoption." Because of, and not in spite of the problem of pain, we will be higher than the angels and archangels, fellow heirs with Jesus Christ. In the first hour of heaven the redeemed can forget all the pain of earth. "I consider that the sufferings of this present time are not worth comparing with the glory that shall be revealed in us" (Romans 8:18).

4

BIND THE STRONG MAN

Lord, send angels and archangels and all the company of heaven to guard and keep us from the evil one. Put the whole armor of God around us that we may be defended in the evil day. Bind the strong man so that Your kingdom may break in with power and great glory.

Jesus, we claim Your victory and Your blood. We thank You that You are in us and that You are stronger than he who is in the world.

Jesus, come quickly in order that the enemy's time may be shortened and his destruction forever stopped. Bind, hinder and confuse every lie and tactic of the enemy. Give us discernment and watchfulness that we may not be tricked or trapped.

Holy Spirit, be the sleepless sentinel that guards our

spirits even when we sleep. May Your flashing sword keep watch over the portals of our lives, so that nothing may enter which is not of Christ. As the flood of the occult threatens to inundate our world and the antichrist cults infiltrate the church itself, claim our nation once more for Christ. Occupy the territory of the enemy through the prayer channels we offer to You now.

In the name of Jesus
Who gave us
access to Your power.

"When a strong man fully armed, guards his palace, his goods are safe; when one stronger than he overcomes him, he takes away his armor and divides his spoil" (Luke 11:21-23). The kingdom of God cannot come at any level until the strong man is first bound. True intercession involves this.

One man who discovered this principle for himself was Johann Christoff Blumhardt. A capable pastor in Moetlingen in the southern part of Germany's Black Forest, he had received his doctorate in theology from the University of Zurich.

In 1842 one his parishioners, a girl named Gottliebin Dittus, began to manifest distressing psychic symptoms. Strange disturbances in the home affected the rest of the family. Mysterious happenings began to be reported elsewhere in the village as well.

Doctor after doctor was called in but not one of them seemed to be able to help poor Gottliebin. Finally a famous neurologist was consulted. He took one look at the afflicted girl and walked over to the parsonage.

"Are there no Christians in this village?" he asked pointedly of Pastor Blumhardt.

Blumhardt somewhat reluctantly undertook the battle. The first time he and Gottliebin prayed together, he said, "Lord Jesus, we have seen long enough what Satan can do, now let us see what You can do."

Thus a battle was joined that lasted nearly two years. Pastor Blumhardt and Gottliebin prayed and sang together almost every day. They read everything that the Bible had to say about the enemy. Many times they sang "A Mighty Fortress Is Our God," especially the lines, "Though devils all the world should fill, they shall not overpower us." Again and again Blumhardt commanded the demons to leave in the name of Jesus. He was inexperienced in this ministry but had a stubborn faith.

Nothing seemed to happen. Meanwhile the whole village was watching and talking. The pastor neglected his parish work. He was growing more tense and tired each day. The manifestations continued and even increased, as if to torment this faithful servant of the Lord. Word was spreading to the outside world, and the curious were beginning to watch the show from outside the house.

As the village looked on, they wondered if Blumhardt's strength or faith would fail before his mind or body gave way. The pressure was building up dangerously. Neighboring pastors were beginning to complain. Every day and every night Blumhardt begged the Lord for more and more grace.

Suddenly and unexpectedly the crisis came. Gottliebin's sister, who was in the room with them, gave a long, rattling cry in a strange voice, "Jesus *ist Sieger*" (Jesus is Victor). It was all over. A legion of demons came rushing out of the Dittus household. That day many people in the village reported the whirring sound of wings and the despairing cry, "Woe, woe, we must go into the abyss!"

"Jesus is Victor" became the battle cry of Blumhardt and his son, Christoff. The victory over the demons that bound Gottliebin led to the breaking in of kingdom power that transformed the life of the entire village. This was renewal beyond anyone's wildest dreams. Lives were transformed, marriages saved, enemies reconciled and lifetime quarrels patched up. It was a spontaneous renewal.

A new note characterized Blumhardt's preaching too. The little village church suddenly became alive. There were outpourings of witness and testimony. Most of all, there were healings. Often when Pastor Blumhardt gave the absolution through the laying on of hands, a healing took place.

Word of the new revival spread. The little church was filled to capacity five times each Sunday, with people often standing outside as far as a kilometer (about 5/8 mile) away. People from the Black Forest region sent their pastors down to be renewed through Blumhardt. One Sunday the German emperor himself came down to see what all the fuss was about.

Although many of Blumhardt's colleagues were dismissed as "Pietists," there was nothing of the fanatic in them. Men like Karl Barth, Emil Brunner, Paul Tillich and Oscar Cullman have numbered them among the greatest theologians of all time. Persecution was their lot and God's countersign was on their ministry.

Satan can counterfeit all the gifts of the Spirit. Wherever the Gospel is plainly spoken, antichrist will build his booth across the street. We live in an age where the snake seems to be gaining ground. Almost all the truly damaging heresies in the church are charismatic heresies such as "Ultimate Reconciliation." How can we tell when and where the strong man is at work? How can he be bound?

The prayer for discernment is one that the Lord answers almost immediately. The prayer is simple:

"Lord, show me what is going on. If this is from You, bless and anoint it. Open the windows of heaven and pour out all your gifts and graces. If this is not from you, bind it and expose it."

I first prayed this prayer a number of years ago in New England. A man who has started several heretical charismatic movements was ministering at a retreat center to which I had been invited. After listening to him for about a half an hour, I walked up and introduced myself by saying, "Brother, you are a false prophet." It was a great way to start a friendship.

That night he was ministering in the chapel with his "charismatic mafia." I was sitting in the back row praying with all my might that the Lord would bind this ministry. After only five minutes he suddenly stopped and announced that there would be no service that night. He and his crew quickly packed up and left.

The prayer for discernment is even more powerful if two intercessors will agree. Once in a charismatic group a brother and I sensed that something was wrong. We prayed for discernment and disclosure. In two days a situation which had been brewing for years was brought out into the open and quickly dealt with.

In this age of phony healers, Eastern mysticism, and the occult, discernment is needed more than ever before. Jehovah's Witnesses, the Mormons, Sun Moon and Yoga are replacing both science and Christianity. We need to know what is going on. We also need to know how to bind it.

The strong man knows the timetable. He knows that his time is strictly limited. Before Christ comes again Satan will concentrate his attack upon those witnesses who are the greatest threat to his kingdom. We never know when or how he is going to attack but we do know that he will. Bind him in the name of Jesus before any of his sneaky plots can get off the ground.

61

Begin every period of sleep and each day with prayer against the enemy, binding his power. (Martin Luther has given us a pattern prayer in his *Morning and Evening Prayers*.) If you do this, Satan will stay away from you and the Spirit's power and blessing will flow unhindered. Once the intercessor has bound the strong man he is free to take all the enemy's spoil. Only when Satan is bound is the kingdom of God free to break in with power and unity. By discernment and intercession we can stake Christ's claim over enemy-occupied territory.

5

DELIVERANCE

Father, if You care for the birds and the lilies, how much more will You also care for us! Because You count the very hairs of our heads, give us the faith to trust You for all things both great and small. Show us that the same Father who provides eternal mansions will also give us temporal food and shelter.

May we seek first the kingdom of God and learn to live one day at a time in Your presence and in Your care. Jesus, give us the peace that the world cannot give and the hope to believe that all things must work together for good for those who truly love You. May yesterday be forgiven and forgotten, today be richly blessed and tomorrow rest in Your perfect plan.

Forgive us for the sin of worry, for majoring in minors and overlooking the kingdom. If we must wor-

ry, let us worry about the right things: Your kingdom and Your righteousness. Father, by the groaning of the Holy Spirit, teach us how to pray. Give us not only the authority but also the power. May we surrender our lives and not just our death into Your hands.

Through Him who was perfectly free to live one day at a time in Your holy will. Amen

At first glance one might wonder what chapters on deliverance are doing in a book on intercession. But Satan dreads nothing more than prayer. The devil flees when he sees a Christian on his knees. But before he flees, he tries in every way to block the prayer.

First, he tries to distract our attention and then to keep us from concentrating. Thoughts and concerns of every kind are put into our minds.

Once a man bet his friend, Charlie, a riding horse that no one could even pray the Lord's Prayer through, without his mind wandering. The bet was on. Charlie began to pray, "Our Father which art in heaven . . . hallowed be Thy name . . . Thy kingdom come . . . Thy will be done on earth as it is in heaven . . . give us . . . will you throw in the saddle, too?"

The weapons of our warfare are spiritual (Ephesians 6:10-19). Most of the armor of God is defensive, but the great offensive weapons are the Word and prayer. "The sword of the Spirit is the Word of God" (v. 17). The greatest offensive weapon is praying in the Spirit. "Pray always in the Spirit with all prayer and supplication. To that end, keep alert, making intercession for all the saints" (v. 18).

If we wait for Satan to attack, he will almost always catch us off guard. We need to go on the offensive and pray against him: "Jesus, come quickly, shorten

Satan's time, hinder his plots, bind and frustrate him at every turn." Or "By the victory and the blood of Jesus, we pray against you, Satan. May all your works and all your ways be exposed and defeated. We claim the almighty name of Jesus against you and all your hosts of darkness. May the Lord deal with you according to His eternal plan and glory. Amen."

The prayer of the Spirit is the sleepless, silent sentinel who guards us even while we sleep. The groaning of the Spirit within us echoes Gethsemane and Calvary. The prayer of the Spirit is God's Spirit praying with and for and in us (Romans 8:26-28).

The Spirit is making intercession through us according to the will of God. He is also praying against the enemy in us and around us.

The whole world is involved in a vast cosmic battle. Deliverance is far more than just casting out demons. Every time someone is healed or freed from sin and bondage, Satan's hold is loosened and God's kingdom begins to break in. This requires an intensive kind of intercession.

Jesus said, "If I cast out demons by the Spirit of God, then the kingdom of God has come upon you" (Matthew 12:28). All of Christ's redeeming activity is a conflict with the devil (Acts 10:38). The Incarnation itself is a result of this clash. Jesus put on flesh and blood to destroy the devil and free those held in bondage by the fear of death (Hebrews 2:14-15).

The battle in the "heavenlies" comes down onto the plains of history and to our own bodies. We are on both sides at once, victor and vanquished, prize and battleground. Yet we cannot see or hear the battle! We can only feel it and observe the ruins in its wake.

Most of the time this battle goes on in a subtle, hidden way. We can only guess at the tremendous spiritual conflicts going on within and around us. A Nativity play once tried to depict this by presenting two scenes at one time. On one stage Satan and the Archangel Michael battled with flashing swords. Behind this scene one could see a man bending over a manger in which a woman was lying on straw. Suddenly the cry of a newborn infant pierced the air. At that very moment Michael ran Satan through with his sword.

When the battle comes out into the open, there are psychic and demonic manifestations. The lowest and most pesky order of these are often called "character demons." They are tremendously difficult to detect because of their close connection with the human will. Satan does many evil things but he also gets blamed for a lot of things that men themselves do.

It is much easier to say, "Satan made me do it," than to admit, "I yielded to temptation and sinned through my own fault." It is far easier to simply have the sin or the habit "cast out" than to repent and exercise self-discipline. When we allow some passion like sex, temper or greed to gain a foothold, we give ground to the enemy. After he has infiltrated our habit patterns, he is extremely hard to detect and dislodge.

One Sunday afternoon I was taking a nap after an especially strenuous morning. I had left instructions with my wife that I didn't want to be disturbed except for an extreme emergency. The phone in my office was turned off. I was lying on the couch with a pillow over my head, deep, deep in well-earned slumber. The other phone rang.

My wife answered and said that I was out—really out. The woman insisted on talking with me anyhow. When Margie said it was impossible, the woman answered, "I've got a gun to my head and I'm going to pull the trigger right now!" Margie gave in.

Groggily, I muttered into the phone, "Yes, what's the problem and who are you, anyhow?"

"Pastor Prange, I'm in hell and you've got to help me! I've been in hell twenty years. You just don't know what it's like!"

"I've been preaching about it for twenty years; maybe I should know a little more about it. Have you been seeing a psychiatrist?" I asked hopefully.

"Oh, yes, for twenty years. He just keeps on saying it's me. I want attention and I was spoiled as a child. But he doesn't know how I feel—he thinks I can help myself. I can't; I don't even want to. I just want to kill myself. Can you help me, Pastor Prange? I must see you right now."

"It's impossible today—my first opening is tomorrow night late. In the meantime, let's have a prayer over the phone so you can hang on until then. Repeat after me, 'I want Jesus to come into my life; I want to be delivered from all evil.' "

The results were explosive and unexpected. Suddenly, I was wide awake and sitting up on the couch.

"No, no! I don't want to be delivered! I don't want Jesus!" The voice was different and coldly menacing.

Demons! What the psychiatrist didn't discover in twenty years and a hundred thousand dollars worth of therapy came out in one phone call. The taunting voice grated across the wire. My whole body was trembling and for some reason I was getting angry. This was no way to spend a sleepy Sunday afternoon.

"You can't cast me out; I'm Lucifer, a high spirit, and you are a mere mortal. I'm the prince of darkness and you're just a two-bit pastor."

"You liar! You are just a private in Satan's army, claiming to be the commanding general himself!"

Soon the demon and I were screaming at each other over the phone. It was unreal! It was wilder even than *The Exorcist*.

"Lucifer, or whoever you are, I am a mere mortal. I

may be a two-bit pastor and I can't cast you out, but I know somebody who can! Jesus! I dare you to bring that woman to the church tomorrow night!"

He fell for the bait. The next night Gloria came with her husband. One look at her was all I needed. She was in hell and somebody from hell was definitely inside of her!

Before the communion rail in church we began the rite of exorcism. "Jesus is Victor. Through the covenant of the Office of the Keys, in His name, and by the power of His blood, I command you to unbind this woman! Name yourself, depart and go to that place that Jesus has assigned for you!" I heard myself shouting as the menacing presence grew stronger.

Suddenly the church was filled with unholy laughter. Gloria began to sneer, "You're a phony, this church is phony, and I don't believe a thing you are saying."

I paid no attention but went on with the rite: "Repeat after me, 'I want to be free, I want Jesus to come into my heart. I renounce the devil and all his works and all his ways.'"

Again the strange anger was welling up inside of me. I wanted to grab her by the throat! Was the demon getting to me, too?

"No, no! I won't and you can't make me!"

"Out, out, in the name of the Lord Jesus!" I began to shout louder.

I felt something begin to leave her. It was rising up in her throat.

"No, no! I don't want it to leave. I won't let go. I don't want to be delivered!" Gloria began to scream.

"That was the last straw," I said. "Look, Gloria, this wasn't my idea in the first place. You woke me out of the best nap I've had in a month of Sundays. You don't even belong to my congregation. You got me out late on my night off. Now, you are going to let go of that demon or I am going to choke him out of you."

"I'll kill myself. I'll kill myself right here in front of your altar. Think of all the publicity!"

She opened her purse and made a sudden move.

"O.K., O.K., you win," I said. "I give up. How did I get into this mess in the first place? It must have been that book I wrote again."

I went into the office and told her husband, "Take her home; there is nothing I can do or God either. Whatever it is has had too strong a hold on her will for too long a time. Gloria and the demon seem to be almost the same person."

At that moment she came out of the church and walked into the office. Her face and neck seemed to have turned to stone. There was a large lump in her throat and she could barely whimper, "Help me, help me." It sounded like the captive soul of the miser in "The Devil and Daniel Webster."

"Will you cooperate this time?" I said, beginning to calm down a bit.

"Yes, yes, anything you say! Just help me!"

This time her husband came along. The demons came out easily and she began to cry.

"Hold me, hold me," she begged like a child.

Her husband held her and we sat in front of the altar rail for over an hour. It was very peaceful. Gloria said it was the first real peace she had known in almost twenty years.

I wish I could report a happy ending but as yet I cannot. The demons were too deeply embedded in Gloria's will. They kept coming back. We have had many sessions together and have checked out all the emotional and psychological dimensions of her life. Through her eyes I have looked into hell many times. I shudder even to say it, but hell is eternal "cold turkey" of the worst kind. I can never doubt its reality now.

One afternoon at the church I wrestled with Satan for an hour for Gloria's soul. It seemed the huge building shook and everyone in it would hear the battle. The enemy withdrew but the deep wounds he left through twenty years will take a long time to heal. For most of her life somebody else has been living through her. The vacuum must be carefully cleaned up and filled. In this case, follow-through is urgent.

Occult demons are more powerful and sometimes create a spectacle when they come out, but they are less attached to the human personality. The occult includes everything from the seemingly harmless psychic to Satan-worship.

Occult deliverance can be dangerous. It is also disturbing. For this reason I try to keep it as private as possible. One night a couple came to our healing service at the church. The man had been involved in the occult, but his wife said that he had given it up and burned all his material.

During the Bible study, he suddenly switched from his high school intellectual level to that of a college professor with three Ph.D.'s. No one could really understand what he was saying, but it sounded terribly erudite to me. The voice was alien and strange. Where did this construction worker suddenly get this tremendous knowledge? A pall fell over the whole meeting. Without even a prayer I dismissed the group and we went into the church.

While I was praying for the sick at the communion rail, this man sat in the back of the church and glared at me. Finally, he shifted his malevolent gaze to the back of a teenager sitting in the front row—Mark Brian, a young black boy on his way to the Air Force. He was a member of the church and we had the best of relationships. He wanted to be prayed for before he reported for military duty.

While Mark was waiting his turn at the altar, a voice whispered in his ear, "When he leans over you, spit in his face." Mark shook his head and pounded on his ear.

The voice came again, this time louder and more insistent, "Better yet, go into his office, get the letter opener out of the upper right-hand drawer and when he lays hands on you, stab him to death."

Like a zombie, Mark got up and headed for my office door. It was locked. He then asked the assistant organist for her key.

"What do you want it for?" Bunny asked. "You have no business in Pastor's private office."

"I want to get the letter opener and kill him."

"What?" Bunny screamed. "Who told you to do such a thing?"

"God told me while I was sitting there on the church bench. It was just as plain as it could be. He even told me what the letter opener looked like."

Bunny managed to get Mark out of the church quietly. Later that night she called me at home and told me what had happened. The letter opener had been gone for three and one-half months and had just been returned that day.

The next morning we had a long talk and an easy deliverance. The episode was over, but I learned again that deliverance was a dangerous form of ministry. Too often new Christians want to flex their spiritual muscles by casting out demons.

Occult spirits can be dormant until there is divine spiritual activity, and then they create extreme personal conflict. One morning the phone rang while I was still at home. The woman at the other end identified herself as Roman Catholic.

"Pastor Prange, I've got to see you right away. It's **really quite urgent!**"

I hesitated.

"Please!"

"All right—just for a few minutes."

We talked for a few minutes in my office at the church. It was an all too typical charismatic tragedy. Gwenn was a practicing Roman Catholic who found her religion satisfying but external and routine. One day she met with a charismatic prayer group. They opened up dimensions of joy and power that she had never dreamed of. The group was Catholic and soon Gwenn, too, received what she had always longed for.

But the honeymoon of the Spirit was all too short. After she fell off the pink cloud, her life began to fall apart. Things were far worse than before. Was this real or some kind of sick joke? Her friends seemed so happy and spiritual, but she grew more desperate each day.

"Can you help me, Pastor Prange? I read your book." (That book again!)

"Tell me a little about your past. Have you ever been involved in the occult?" I asked her.

"Yes, a long time ago. I got pretty involved, I suppose, but I've given it all up."

"Have you ever confessed this and received absolution and deliverance?"

"No, do I have to do that?"

"That, plus burning all your materials and breaking all your contacts, is the only sure way to be free," I said, remembering my own experience.

All at once Gwenn changed, right in front of my eyes. She had been friendly and even charming, but now there was a threat in her eyes and voice. She leaned toward me.

"I feel like calling you every dirty, filthy, vile name I can think of—you—you . . . "

"Let's get into the church fast," I said, grabbing her by the arm.

Before the altar I began to pray. After the prayers of protection and challenge, I asked, "Who are you? Name yourself."

Gwenn began to scream, "I'm not who you think I am—there are a lot of us in here!"

"Come out then, in the name of Jesus, all of you!" I ordered.

A gale of hysterical laughter filled the church. It sounded like children. Gwenn became ill, right on the leather kneelers.

Unexpectedly, she reached for my throat. It took all my strength to hold her wrists. Pretty soon we were all yelling.

Just at that moment the Wednesday morning Bible class walked down the hallway of the annex. At first they thought the church was full of mischievous children. Then they heard my voice. They asked the assistant pastor what I was doing.

"Oh, I think Pastor Prange is counseling with a woman in the church."

"Well! I never heard any counseling like that in my whole life!" two of them said.

The charismatics in the Bible class looked at each other knowingly. They had already felt the goose pimples rising on their skin.

In the church there was sudden silence. Gwenn became limp. She was weak but the battle was over.

That day we buried the former pastor of the church. That night I performed the wedding of my eldest daughter. I came over two hours before the wedding and tried to clean the church out. People kept interrupting me and following me around.

"What are you doing, Pastor? Why are you making the sign of the cross everywhere? What are you mumbling?"

How do you tell innocent people, getting ready for a

wedding, that you are cleaning demons out of the church?

The most powerful of all demons are the religious ones. This is the antichrist pattern. They come in the name of Christ and undermine everything He stands for. Jehovah's Witnesses, Children of God, and many others belong to this group. Religious demons are exceedingly dangerous and exert some kind of strange influence over their victims. It is a trance-like state similar to hypnosis and drugs but far more persistent.

When the Korean "Messiah" came to Baltimore, I counseled with some of his followers who were of German and Austrian nationality. We talked together and prayed together in German. I tried healing, exorcism and intercession, but nothing helped. One day after praying for an hour with an Austrian Jesuit who was part of the movement, I said in German, *"Sie sind wie im Traum."* (You are in something like a dream state.)

"Yawohl," he said, and left. I never saw him again.

But I did see his boss. One Sunday morning a medium-sized man in a grey suit walked into the adult Bible class. Why did he look so hauntingly and frighteningly familiar?

"I know that man," I said to myself. "I've seen him a thousand times. He's everybody and he's nobody, he's—no, I won't even think it!"

He came into my office right before the sermon and tried to promote the Korean "Messiah" again. I had to rush out and catch up with the choir procession. Halfway up the aisle, I remembered who he was. That morning, nothing went right. The candles wouldn't light, the choir couldn't sing, and we kept dropping the communion wafers. Somehow, we bumbled and bungled through the service.

One Friday night after a sensational newspaper article on deliverance had quoted me, we had another visitor. He was skinny and birdlike. He refused to join the circle or to pray with us. He just sat in the back and kept muttering to himself. Suddenly he was gone and we could pray again.

Warning signs of evil spiritual activity are non-rational, subclinical depression and an irrational resistance to the Word of God. Sudden explosive emotional displays, compulsive behavior and a deep split in will and motivation are suspect. God is love and His presence brings peace and joy. The enemy is hate and his presence brings depression and destruction. God is a God of order; the demonic is utterly irrational. Intensive intercession alone is able to cope with the enemy.

6

INTERCESSION

Holy Spirit, we do not know how to pray. We, in our ignorance, can only spoil God's perfect plan for us. So, pray within us with sighs and groans too deep for words or thoughts. Plug us in to that great cosmic prayer chain where angels and archangels and all the company of heaven continuously chant the wonders of Jesus' love.

Jesus, pray to the Father for us. He always hears You and can refuse You nothing. Father, Son and Holy Spirit, teach us also to pray with and for You that we may take our eyes off ourselves. You have made us for only one reason: to be containers of the Divine Life. Fill us now with that Life from the soles of our feet to the crowns of our heads.

Jesus, let Your light and love and truth now flow

*into every cell and atom and electron of our bodies.
Jesus, make us true intercessors who pray in Your
name and manner. Let us be willing to take the other's
place as You take ours. Show us that we can claim
nothing from You except Your mercy and Your love.
Before we offer ourselves for others, may we first
place that total self on Your altar. As You have freely
and totally given Yourself to us, accept our lives as
living sacrifices.*

*In the name of Him
Who tasted death for
all men—Jesus. Amen.*

For two years we held a healing service each Friday
night at our church in Baltimore, a beautiful stone
cathedral located just two blocks from Memorial
Stadium. On the nights that the Colts or the Orioles
played, traffic and parking often became a tangled
nightmare. People came from Virginia, Washington,
D.C., New York, Florida and even Guatemala.

Because we were only a few blocks from the deep
ghetto, many local people were afraid to come. The
blacks, who formed about half of the congregation,
were especially afraid because they had to go home to
the worst neighborhoods.

Though our numbers were often relatively small, the
Lord continued to lead us forward into deeper and
deeper insights. Physical healing became almost
routine. Sometimes, bafflingly, nothing seemed to
happen, even though we prayed fervently week after
week. It was as if God was trying to point beyond
physical healing to something far more important.
After a while it became apparent that those who were
healed, as well as those who were not, had been
changed.

What years of preaching and teaching had not been

able to accomplish, sometimes happened in a moment to those who presented themselves in humility and faith before God's throne. Was there something to the theology of decision after all? One could be a faithful church member for ninety years and a pastor for sixty without ever making a real commitment to Christ! Was God using physical healing as a way to get men and women on their knees?

Even the little children who came with their parents to the communion rail for blessing were changed. If they had not yet been confirmed, I would give each one a personal blessing with the laying on of hands. Sometimes they even remembered the blessing and repeated it to their parents at home. They prayed out loud, they witnessed, and they loved—something that few adults had learned to do!

From physical healing we moved easily into healing of the emotions and memories. My counseling became largely a healing of relationships. But the Lord seemed to be leading in a different direction. I couldn't get Rees Howells out of my mind. What about intercession? Were those of us who had been meeting together for almost four years ready to become a team of intercessors?

Why should intercession be so powerful? After all, we were just a handful of people in a terribly messed-up world.

I remembered a time back in Germany, right after the war had ended. The United States had just dismantled its mighty army but the Russian giant was still intact, poised like a sword over the heart of Europe. My commanding officer, Colonel Smith, was called to a top-secret meeting at 2:00 A.M. The next day he told me what had been discussed.

"How bad is it, Colonel?" I asked.

"Erve, if you look out of your window some morning

and see the Hammer and Sickle instead of the Stars and Stripes, don't be surprised. Don't try to go anywhere either; we are expendable."

"I don't mind dying that much, Colonel, but from the stories I've heard, Siberia is no place for a Texan."

Years later I was to find out what apparently saved us on that fateful night: Russia thought we might have as many as a hundred atomic bombs when actually we had only two!

If the fate of the world hung by such slender threads, how much more might the chain of intercession suspend our destinies? God was indeed leading us toward intercession, but just how? Were all those mysteries and happy accidents but "a shade of His hand outstretched caressingly"?

The "Sanctus" in the communion service provided a liturgical key to the vast power of intercession. "Therefore, with angels and archangels and with all the company of heaven, we laud and magnify Thy glorious name." We do not pray just as individuals; we can plug into that vast cosmic chain of intercession and praise.

When we pray as the Body of Christ, God does not see us kneeling alone, swallowed up in an infinite universe. He sees His beloved Son reaching out with nail-pierced hands in total love and perfect obedience.

It was easy to see, theologically, why intercession was so powerful. God prays with us. The Spirit prays in the unsearchable depths of our hearts with sighs and groans too deep for words (Romans 8:26-27). Jesus also makes constant intercession for us from the right hand of the Father. With the Son and Holy Spirit praying for us and through us, how can we lose?

God not only prays for us, He also asks us to pray for Him. Religion is either theocentric or egocentric. That is, we either focus on God or on ourselves. In the Lord's

Prayer, God asks us to focus on Him by praying for Him. "Hallowed be *Thy* name, *Thy* kingdom come, *Thy* will be done." There is not a single petition that asks that we become more sanctified.

In Matthew 9:38, Jesus asks that we pray the Lord of the harvest that He might send workers into His harvest. Why should we pray for God to send workers into His own harvest? If it is His will, won't He see that it gets done? Why should we interfere in His business? He wants us to take our minds off ourselves and focus on Him.

In Colossians 4:3, Paul asks us to pray for the Word. God wants us to pray for His Word in order that we might become a part of it. As it goes out through us and comes back with fruit, we get a double blessing. God knows our subjectivity; He wants us to be a vital part of His eternal objectivity.

Family Covenant

The first breakthrough began with the "family covenant." This was based on Acts 16:31, "You will be saved and your household." Most problems brought to a pastor are family problems. "What can I do about my husband? My wife? My children?"

Carl and Stephen were seventeen and fifteen years old when they first came to me to talk about their alcoholic mother.

"Pastor, it's getting worse and worse. We can't talk to her about it. She hides it and then she denies it. Sometimes I think she must drink as much as a quart a day," Carl, the eldest, related.

"She comes to church regularly. Would it help if I talked to her?" I asked.

"I don't think so. She doesn't like you for some reason. I think she's afraid of you. Maybe she thinks you have too much influence over us. If she even knew we were here now talking to you, she might never show up around here again."

"Well, I guess we'll have to sneak up on her," I said.

"What do you mean by that, Pastor?"

"I'll pray the family covenant every Friday night with both of you until God says 'yes,' 'no,' or 'shut up.'"

Carl and Stephen were wonderful boys. Every Friday night I laid hands on both of them and we prayed for their mother. First Carl and then Stephen received the baptism with the Holy Spirit in the process of intercession. At first not much seemed to be happening.

One Friday they reported that she had tapered off a little. Then she began to conceal it more carefully. She didn't know we were praying but the Spirit was placing her under conviction. Once she stopped for a week and then started again, heavier than ever. We kept on praying for over a year and then suddenly the drinking ceased. The victory was won and to this day Mrs. Roth does not know that she was being prayed for.

Proxy Prayers

With the family covenant we began to move more and more into the area of proxy prayers. In this kind of intercession relatives and friends come forward and offer themselves as proxies for sick relatives and acquaintances. Proxy prayers include every kind of need: spiritual, physical, emotional and mental. In a true proxy prayer the proxy should know the sick person well, should care enough to be an intercessor, should be a fitting proxy and willing to be used as an answer to his own prayer.

When we pray through proxies we need to be able to visualize the sick person as concretely and compassionately as possible. In our "prayer eye," we ought to be able to see Jesus touching and healing. In the case of a child or a desperately ill person we try to see and even feel ourselves carrying the afflicted one into the light of Jesus' healing presence. The proxy form of intercession is a way of healing relationships and of healing the human spirit. The wounds may be so deep and hidden that there is no direct way of approaching the sufferer.

John had been in deep depression and had undergone shock treatment a number of times. He came to our Friday night meetings and was beautifully healed. After about a year he began to regress again. Doctors, psychiatrists, medicines and prayers, nothing seemed to help any more. That finally left only one possibility, but neither he nor his wife were open to the suggestion of possible demonic bondage.

Lloyd had been with our prayer group for four years and had himself come out of deep, suicidal depression. He was in a mental hospital when he found the Lord and was healed. We had grown spiritually together and shared the same revelations about intercession. Lloyd also had been given a marvelous ministry to two inner city nursing homes.

One Friday night as I prayed at the altar for the sick, I heard Lloyd in the back of the church praying for John. He laid hands on him and said, "Lord, I know what this kind of depression is like; it's hell itself. You once rescued me from it. Now I pray that You would put whatever is on John upon me. Let me take his place in this awful agony."

I knew that Lloyd meant every word he said and also understood the implications of what he was praying. So I wasn't surprised when his wife called the next Wednesday and reported that he had gone into deep depression. He had gone back almost to the point where he had been in the hospital. Everything seemed to be falling apart in front of our eyes, his life, his faith and his marriage.

We made an appointment for that night in the church. At the altar Lloyd began to tremble violently and when I laid hands on him he passed out cold for several minutes. After he had come to, he was fine and has remained so ever since.

The next day I called John. "How are you, anyhow?" I asked.

"It's funny that you should ask, Pastor. I had a terrible weekend and then suddenly last night I felt better. Today I feel great."

"What do you know, it works!" I muttered to myself again. "I keep telling people all these things. I'm glad someone has the courage to believe and the guts to try them. Or else how would I ever know if they were true or not?"

I remember a woman who had come to me in Minneapolis at a convention. I was leading the healing workshop. After the presentation, people began to line up for prayers. One woman kept trying to get to the head of the line. She sent emergency messages and notes but I replied, "Send her away for she crieth after us."

Finally, she did make it to the head of the line. Then she unfolded a scroll that seemed to be a yard long. It was a list of prayers and intercessions that included every need in her own life and that of all her family and friends.

I groaned in spirit. "Do you expect me to pray for all of those things, right here and now?"

"Of course, Pastor, isn't that what you are here for?"

"Do you believe that God is going to answer all of those prayers?"

"Of course. Don't you?"

She had me there. So we prayed through the whole

list. I've forgotten most of the prayers but I do remember one about a nephew who had been hospitalized as a hopeless schizophrenic for twenty years. I also seem to remember something about her husband being very sick.

Six months later at Ann Arbor I ran into a pastor from her home town.

"Do you remember the lady with the list?" he asked.

"You mean the woman from Tyre and Sidon? How could I ever forget her?" I groaned, just recalling the length of that list.

"Do you know that the Lord answered every prayer on her list?"

"Every prayer?" I was incredulous.

"When she got home, her husband was well. She didn't seem to be at all surprised. Then she asked, 'Where is my nephew?' "

" 'Oh,' her husband said, 'the hospital just called, they are sending him home, he's cured.' "

So it went on down the list. "What do you know! It really works," I exclaimed. What was different about this woman and her list? Was it faith? She really bugged me. Are we supposed to bug God? I wish I knew the answer.

There is something terribly subjective about answered prayer and healing miracles. Sometimes we need solid, unambiguous evidence. Men do not pray because of fear or hope but because of convincing personal witness.

At a leadership conference in Ann Arbor, Michigan, in February 1973 I had the healing workshop. Most of those in the workshop were pastors. After my presentation, I asked those who wanted ministry to come forward. No one stirred. I felt terribly rejected. Finally, an orthopedic surgeon from California gave a beautiful testimony about the healing of his own back through prayer. Still no one came forward for ministry.

"What's the matter," I asked, "is no one sick or do you lack faith?"

"It's just that we have never seen a healing by prayer," one pastor volunteered.

"That's no problem," I said. Then I sent my assistant out to bring in two people with short legs. Pretty soon he came back with two people in tow who were wearing built-up shoes. They seemed to be somewhat reluctant and confused.

"Sit here in front," I said and proceeded to take off their shoes. The pastors were watching, fascinated. We prayed and suddenly the legs were lengthened. Still no one stirred.

"That's a good trick," I heard someone in the back say. "In a little while those legs will shrink again. I've heard about this."

"Oh, ye of little faith!" I muttered to myself. Just when I was ready to give up, a tall distinguished-looking layman stepped forward.

"Pray for my back, Pastor," he said.

When he came forward, his pastor followed somewhat reluctantly. He told me that he had a terrible fear of death based on a diagnosis of possible leukemia. Almost all the males in his family had died of cancer.

After he had come forward, other pastors followed. We began to pray. It seemed that they were all being healed, like ducks in a row.

That night the layman who had led the parade invited me to have dinner with a group of his friends. After dinner we met in his hotel room for prayer. Every prayer spoken in his room on that night was answered. I prayed by proxy for a nineteen-year-old boy with cancer of the bone. I had never seen him in my life and still haven't.

Almost two years later at Minneapolis the layman, a senior engineer for a large corporation, gave his testimony. When they returned to Ann Arbor, his pastor had gone to Mayo Clinic in Rochester for another checkup. Before going to Ann Arbor, fifteen negative factors had been discovered in his blood. This time there were none. The head of the clinic himself came to see the pastor and asked for an explanation. Pastor Petersen gave his testimony.

"You really believe that, don't you?" the doctor asked skeptically.

"Yes. Do you have a better explanation, doctor?"

"No, I don't frankly. Now you can help me."

"How?" Pastor Petersen asked.

"I'm scheduled for open-heart surgery and I'm scared. Pray for me. The power that cleared up your blood can also heal my heart."

They prayed together. When Pastor Petersen left, the doctor did not present him with a bill. "We have ministered to each other," he said simply.

Before the Ann Arbor meeting the young man we prayed for by proxy had also come to the Mayo Clinic. His illness was diagnosed as cancer of the bone. A bone chip had been removed for biopsy and now the surgeons wanted to remove his arm and shoulder bone. However, the family was told that even that wouldn't help. The doctors at Mayo finally leveled with them and said that so far in medical history no one had ever survived that kind of cancer for more than a year.

Jim and his family refused surgery. Chemo- and radiotherapy were begun but the reactions were so intense that therapy was discontinued. In the meantime the various prayer groups in Jim's church continued in intercession. There was prophecy and also a word about Ann Arbor.

After the prayer in the hotel room at Ann Arbor, Jim

went back to Mayo for another checkup. Numerous X-rays were taken. Finally the chief orthopedic surgeon called Jim into his office.

"Jim," he said, "if I didn't know your history and you had just walked in off the street, I would say this: sometime in the past a small bone chip was removed from your shoulder. Presumably it was for some kind of test. However, on the basis of the most recent X-rays, I would not be able to say what the doctors were looking for. There is no evidence of any abnormality in your bone or other tissues. There is also no evidence in the X-rays that anything has ever been abnormal in your physiological structure."

True prayer and real intercession are guided. They are given by God. Through the Spirit, His will is seeking a concrete channel for expression and fulfillment.

At the first Ann Arbor leadership conference, a pastor approached me. Overshadowed would be a better word since he was a giant of a man. He looked like a descendant of the mighty Vikings of old. But he was a Viking with a flaw.

"Pastor Prange, three times the Lord has told me to have you pray for me—once in Minneapolis, another time in Denver and now here. Frankly, I'm afraid; what should I do?"

"Tell me," I said, "did God call me by name? The enemy usually says 'him,' 'that man,' or far worse."

"Yes, the voice used your name all three times."

"Then, what are you afraid of?"

"Well, I was prayed for once before by a prayer group. I got worse and almost died. In the hospital the medicine worked in exactly the opposite way that it was supposed to. My doctor was discerning enough to suspect demonic influence and called for a ministry of deliverance. So, you see, that's why I'm afraid to be prayed for again."

"I understand," I said. "How big a diabetic problem do you have?"

"For twenty years I've been injecting some sixty units per day."

"What are we waiting for? When God commands, we must obey. He's told you three times now. He might not give you another chance. Let's go into the prayer room right now." I, too, had received the command. There was no time for lingering or for doubting.

We went into the prayer room. As the blond giant knelt before me, I could almost stand up straight and look him right in the eye. The Lord gave us the prayer that had been trying so long to get through. The words came bursting out. God was praying and answering His own prayer at the same time! But He was doing it through us!

When we walked out of the prayer room Pastor Nelson had feeling in his feet for the first time in twenty-five years. But now we had another problem—what to do about his insulin shots?

The thorniest question in divine healing is: why are some healed and not others? The second most difficult problem is: what to do about physical medicine?

"Pastor Prange, shall I keep on taking insulin? We have both had confirmation of my healing. Shall I just claim it by faith and take the risk of going into a diabetic coma?"

I knew that many healing ministries had been shot down just on this issue. I prayed silently for a minute or two.

"I cannot tell you to take medicine or not to take it. That is not my ministry. Try cutting down slowly and let God and your doctor be your guides." That was the safe way out but the Lord was also protecting my ministry.

The next day I saw Pastor Nelson. Before I could ask

him how he felt, he told me this story, "This morning I started to give myself the slow-acting insulin. I usually inject that first and then afterward the fast-acting kind. I had prayed all night about it but wasn't sure just what the Lord wanted me to do. For the second time in twenty years I broke a bottle. This time it seemed to almost leap out of my hand. It shattered in a thousand pieces against the wall. Now what shall I do?"

"I think God has given you your answer. He must give it to you personally. I cannot. The enemy would dearly love to compromise my healing ministry," I replied.

I have not yet heard the end of this story. Perhaps the end is not as important as the lessons we learned. Sometimes I may indulge in medical diagnosis but I never, never give medical advice. Jesus is the great and only physician. Sometimes He uses me as His channel for healing. How He uses His many other channels is simply not my business.

Keep On Praying

We keep on praying until the Lord says, "yes," "no" or "shutup." "But the Lord was angry with me on your account, and would not listen to me; and the Lord said to me, 'Enough! Speak to Me no more of this matter'" (Deuteronomy 3:26).

George Muller is a perfect example of the process of intercession. When the Lord laid something on his heart he did not stop praying until the answer came. According to his diary the Lord specifically answered fifty thousand prayers in his life, five thousand of them before he got off his knees. However, many of his prayers were not answered during his lifetime. They continued to be answered almost one hundred years after his death!

Rees Howells is another perfect illustration of the process of intercession. For five years during World

War II, the Lord revealed to him step by step and day by day the process of intercession.

To pray once and forever after claim the healing by faith goes against many Biblical examples. The woman from Tyre and Sidon, the friend coming at midnight, and the woman who pestered the unjust judge are examples of persistence in prayer. God wants us to ask and to keep on asking. He wants eternal relationship; we want immediate physical help. He may keep us on our knees and before His throne until the entire healing is completed—physical, emotional and spiritual.

Mrs. Miller was an R.N. and the wife of a retired Baltimore Colts tackle. She suffered from severe scoliosis or deformation of the spine and had undergone several serious and painful operations.

The first time she came to our healing service, she received healing for her lower back. The next time there was some further physical healing, but the major problem still persisted.

As we continued to pray, the Lord began to deal with her spiritual life. Then He began to work out her relationships. However, the scoliosis continued and the pain seemed to be getting worse. Her orthopedic surgeon told her there was no real hope for recovery. "Just bite the bullet and accept it," he said.

"I refuse," Mrs. Miller replied stubbornly.

"Then what are you going to do?"

"God is going to heal me."

She ended up with a psychiatrist.

"Look," he said, "you are a nurse. You know the diagnosis and the prognosis. Now be realistic. Accept your disease and take as many pain killers as possible."

"Is that all you can tell me? Is that all that medicine has to offer? There has got to be a better answer and I'm determined to find it."

She made an appointment with me. The day she was

91

to come was rainy and stormy. She called and said that she had the flu but still wanted to come.

"No," I said, "stay right there in bed. This is the day the Lord has appointed to heal you and He can do it over the phone just as well."

Before we prayed I asked her to lay her hand on the lump on her back.

We prayed on the phone, "Jesus, You have no hands and feet or voice in the world but ours. Shut out the image of ourselves and become incarnate in this prayer. Let the hand on Mrs. Miller's back be Yours. May the voice over the wire be Yours also.

"Let the fingers that put the galaxies in place reach deep down inside that spine and rearrange the muscles, nerves and bones. Speak the word that made the heaven and the earth, in order that this body may be recreated. Make the temple of this body whole and holy, that Your will may be done perfectly through it."

The anointing was so heavy it seemed the phone wires would melt. We both had the overwhelming conviction that Mrs. Miller was healed at that moment.

The pain ceased immediately. The remission lasted for three weeks. Mrs. Miller began to give her testimony to anyone who would listen. But she made one big mistake. There was one more lesson to learn.

"I went everywhere looking for help, even to Kathryn Kuhlman, but the only one who ever did me any good was Pastor Prange. His prayers healed me when nothing else could." She went around everywhere singing my praises.

Then, wham! The symptoms came back worse than before. All her great testimony fell flat. The doctors were saying, "I told you so." Her husband lost what little faith he had in divine healing.

She called and told her story, "I just can't understand, Pastor Prange. God has dealt with everything in my life. I thought it was all behind me and now this."

"There's just one more thing," I said.

"What's that?" she asked.

"You forgot to give God the glory. He will not share His glory with another. You've been going around singing my praises instead of glorifying God. Stop it before you get us both into deep trouble."

She began to praise God and stopped even mentioning my name. The symptoms and the pain departed. Her face shone with new health and life. She didn't even have to testify. People took one look at her and asked, "What in the world has happened to you?" God had finally completed the job He wanted to do on her—and on me, too.

Intercession is costly. It cost Jesus His life. It costs us all of ourselves. This is the third stage of the cross. The first two—salvation and sanctification—may be egocentric. The desire for personal salvation is basically self-centered. Sanctification can also be selfish. It may be a drive for power and status, a kind of spiritual ego trip.

Intercession is different. It goes out from ourselves toward others. It is a way of pouring the resurrection life of Christ into the world. The intercessor is a channel for the blessings of the ascended Lord. The intercessor must be, like Christ, willing to take the other's place and even to give his life.

The true intercessor can claim nothing for himself. Jesus was not allowed to use His power to turn stones into bread or to come down from the cross. Paul said, "We are poor, yet making many rich. Death works in us but life in You." In Colossians, he says, "The sufferings of Christ are completed in His body, the Church."

Only when the intercessor renounces his claims on God, is God free to answer his prayers. Our claims upon

God are always based upon the Word and never upon ourselves. We cannot say, for example, "God, you owe me this," or "You ought to do this because of what I have done for You." This is the great temptation of the intercessor, to lay claim to his own merit or work.

The right kind of intercession is infinitely powerful. One man, C.T. Studd, prayed the Gospel into Africa. Praying Hyde, by groans and tears of intercession, brought the Gospel to India, and Hudson Taylor, to China. St. Francis, by his intercession, saved the medieval church. This kind of praying is the key to the survival of the Church and the world.

The heart of God is breaking. He wants to bless a thousand times and heal ten thousand times. He holds a million unclaimed gifts in the storehouse of His mercy. But He cannot find intercessors to deliver them.

7

PATTERNS OF INTERCESSION

King of kings and Lord of lords, You have made us in Your image. We are not spectators of the divine drama but partners with You through prayer. Forgive us for taking You for granted, for neglecting this great power of ministry. May we see that every lungfull of air and every heartbeat are personal gifts from You. Let every moment of time be filled with all the eternal possibility that You have placed into it.

Jesus, beat in our hearts, flow in our blood, think in our minds, walk in our feet. Let us have Your mind and think God's thoughts after Him. Father, Son and Holy Spirit, may the divine image breathed into us twice be realized through creative prayer.

Jesus, teach us to pray as You taught Your disciples. May we pray in the great patterns that You have laid down in Your Word. May the angels and archangels mingle our prayers with incense from the heavenly altar and carry them straight to the highest throne of God.

Holy Spirit, You do not have a body; use ours as Your temple. Father, as You were once incarnate in Jesus of Nazareth, become incarnate all over the world through our intercession and thanksgiving. Forgive us the wasted hours and years. Free us from all hurtful habits and careless living that hinder and cut short Your eternal plan for every moment of our lives. Whither shall we flee from Your presence. Search us and know us, O God!

In the name of Him
Who makes it possible to
pray, "Our Father."

The Prayer of Elijah
The intercessions of Jesus and those of the Old Testament prophets were much different from our own. They were actually prophetic declarations rather than petitions. All the preliminaries had been worked out with God in advance.

Instead of "Please God, if it is Your will," these great men of prayer simply declared, "So shall it be." Elijah said, "It shall not rain for three and one-half years," and it didn't. Isaiah said to Hezekiah, "You shall live and not die," and he lived. It was as simple as that.

It is hard for the average praying Christian to identify with these Biblical heroes of the faith. Yet the New Testament prayer model laid down for us is exactly this type of prayer. "The prayer of a righteous man has great power in its effects. Elijah was a man of like nature with ourselves, and he prayed fervently that it might not rain, and for three years and six months it did not rain upon the earth. Then he prayed again and the heaven gave rain and the earth brought forth its fruit" (James 5:16-18).

These are the key passages on intercession in the Bible. First of all Elijah is identified with us, "like nature as ourselves." Every intercessor has his potential; if not, he has a track record. Elijah is called a righteous man because he had a right prayer relationship with God. "Effectual fervent prayer" means bold, believing intercession. Elijah with his head bowed down on the mountain side also presented the classic image of prayer for the Jews.

Prayer changes things. It can even change the weather because we are not mere helpless spectators at the drama of creation; we are co-creators with God through intercessory prayer. This is the real meaning of the image of God.

In the uncreated middle, between God's absolute sovereignty and the rebellion of sin, we are part of the creating Word. Many things could happen but do not because we fail to claim this power. "You have not because you ask not" (James 4:2). God wants to give us many things, but most of His blessings lie unclaimed in the "heavenly dead-letter office."

God certainly is able. He is also more than willing. We have at our disposal the same Word that created the heavens and the earth. The fingers that put the galaxies in place are also clasped in our own. The power that broke open the tomb on Easter morning dwells within us. It's not that we ask too much. We are pikers begging for trifles, when God wants to give us all things.

In the summer of 1974 we decided to try the prayer pattern of Elijah. My wife and I with our two daughters drove to my old home in west Texas to visit my mother and sisters. Normally dry, the area around Cisco had become a semi-desert. Lakes and ponds were almost empty, the seed was blowing out of the fields and it looked as if another dust bowl might be in the making.

My sister, Chris, and I went to visit a member of her prayer group in a nearby town. Ria is part Hungarian, part Cuban, part Jewish and the rest charismatic. Her husband and father-in-law are both refugee Cuban doctors. They live in a large house on a beautiful private lake. The only problem was, the lake was almost dry.

As we looked over the dry lake bed, Ria asked, "What can we do about this?"

Without thinking, I said, "Let's just pray the prayer of Elijah."

"How do you do that?" Ria asked.

"We'll check it out in the Old Testament and in James and do exactly what it says." I wasn't nearly as confident as I sounded. I had never tried it before but this dry, rocky lake looked like a perfect place to start. It even had a mountain side that I could bury my face against and a cave to crouch in, just like Elijah's.

Chris, Ria and I joined hands, buried our faces in the rock hillside and boldly declared that it would rain. Just then Ria's father-in-law walked by. He paused for a moment and I'm sure he was trying to think of a good psychiatrist to call.

When we had finished praying Ria asked, "Now what about Lake Cisco?"

We got into the car, stopped by and picked up Margie and then headed for Lake Cisco. When the water was close to spillway level, Lake Cisco had a shoreline over a hundred miles long. It is located in a ruggedly beautiful, rocky setting. For several years, while manager of Cisco Country Club, I had lived on one of its steep crags. In over forty years I had never seen the water level so low. It was a pitiful, sickening sight. Again we joined hands and our faces to the ground on the side of the rocky lake road.

"In the name of the living God we declare that it shall rain and this lake will be filled, according to the prayer of Elijah and by the power of Jesus Who creates and upholds all things."

People who knew us began to drive by and stare. I could almost hear them saying, "Erve Prange is finally cracking up. He was a good ole country boy once, but he just stayed too long in them big cities in the East. It'll get to you finally; too bad."

"Lord we claim the promise of the prayer of Elijah. Even though there isn't a cloud the size of a man's hand in the whole sky, we can already hear the sound of a mighty rain. So be it, in Jesus' name, Amen."

Soon afterward we drove to a conference in Minneapolis, Minnesota, where I was to conduct a workshop on healing. Before we got there the rains came to Texas. It rained for forty days and forty nights. Some old-timers claimed that it rained more than during Noah's flood. It rained more in four months than it had during the previous ten years. The lakes filled and the fields were flooded.

My brother-in-law, Ernest, had been the biggest scoffer of all. His peanut farm and cattle ranch are located about seven miles south of Cisco and about ten miles from Ria's place near Baird, Texas. He kept needling me before we went to Minneapolis.

"It'll never rain now, especially in Baird. You've ruined what little chance we had. Those lakes are going to get so dry that even the fish will have to walk. How did you talk Chris into this anyhow? There's not a cloud even near Baird or Lake Cisco. Why don't you just call Ria and see if they have had so much as one drop of rain since you prayed?"

It was the prophets of Baal all over again. This was a good sign.

I could tease too. "I tried to call Ria but all that came

over the phone was 'gurgle, gurgle, gurgle.' They must be having an awful flood by now. Maybe we should send boats and have Baird declared a disaster flood area."

So it went until we left. In November back in Baltimore, Ernest and I talked over the phone, long distance.

"Okay, okay," he said, "you win, but now how do you turn it off? I need to get into my fields to harvest my crops."

"I'm sorry," I said, "but this kind takes three years and six months."

"By that time we'll all be drowned," he groaned.

It rained normally in Texas for almost a year. Then it became very dry again. My sister, Chris, and I talked about it on the phone. The beautiful peanut crop that I had admired in August was about to burn up. I told Chris to pray the prayer of Elijah once more. She did and again the rains came just in time.

Baltimore needs the other half of the prayer of Elijah. It rains almost every day and especially on Sunday. Our Sunday School picnic was scheduled for the second Sunday in June. It had been pouring almost every Sunday so at the planning meeting the question came up, "What if it rains?"

Elijah Prange suddenly spoke up, "It shall not rain." There was an embarrassed silence.

"Are you sure?" they all chorused.

"Yes, I guarantee it. I'm praying the prayer of Elijah."

"We'll hold you responsible if it does."

It did not rain but it almost snowed. One of our members, a senior engineer, told the story at work. One of his colleagues said, "That pastor of yours has just got to be the most insufferable egotist who ever lived."

"No," Bob said, "he just has a funny thing about prayer."

On July 3rd, 1975, a rock concert was scheduled at Memorial Stadium just two blocks from our house. The Stadium Task Force and other community organizations were trying to get an injunction to stop it. I signed the petition because more and more the concert began to look like a combination of Woodstock and the Watts riots.

Nothing helped. At five o'clock on the evening of July 3rd, the first ticket holders of an advance sale of over twenty thousand began to arrive. They were a raunchy looking lot and we braced ourselves for what surely must be coming. I decided not to go calling that night but to ride shotgun on the place with our two boys.

As I sat looking out my office window at the campers and the liberated acid rock fans, I thought again of the prayer of Elijah.

"Lord, You know this is going to be an unmitigated disaster," I prayed. "Last time there was a terrible race riot and some people were pushed from the top of the stadium and killed. It took months to clean up afterwards. Now let a storm come and let it rain and stop this concert."

In a few minutes a strong wind blew up and it began to rain. The wind blew the extra light bars down from the top of the stadium and hot wires were popping all over the wet grass. No one seemed to know how to turn off the power. The concert was called off. The rain and the wind ceased. The promoter lost fifty thousand dollars. I hope he never reads this book or I will surely be sued.

Coincidence? Maybe. Praise the Lord, anyhow, and be careful how you pray. He just might answer.

The Family Covenant Prayer

God sees families as tied together spiritually. "And they said, 'Believe in the Lord Jesus, and you will be saved, you and your household' " (Acts 16:31). About 98 percent of the problems brought to my attention as a pastor are family problems. People in families are deeply involved with each other. This involvement is total and eternal. "Obey your leaders and submit to them; for they are keeping watch over your souls, as men who will have to give account" (Hebrews 13:17).

The family is the basic cell of the church (Ephesians 5:21-33). In the Old Testament the father in each family was also its priest. This role is still observed today in much of Judaism.

One of the key concepts of the Bible is in the "covenant" or "testament." The Hebrew word is *berith* and the Greek *diatheke*. God is a covenant God and all His promises are covenant promises. Covenant is not a negotiated agreement between two parties but God's sovereign and free declaration about His way of relating to us.

In the Old Testament, circumcision of the males was an outward sign of the covenant. In the New Testament, the sign is water baptism. The Old Testament covenant was one of law regulated by an external code. This code was symbolized by the Ten Commandments and the two tablets of stone. The New Testament covenant is the Gospel, or good news of grace through faith in Jesus Christ.

The new covenant is internal. Its sign is the presence of the Holy Spirit within us. "The days will come says the Lord when I will establish a new covenant with the house of Israel not like the covenant I made with their fathers ... This is the covenant I will make ... I will put my law into their minds, and write it on their hearts, and I shall be their God and they shall be My people. And they shall not teach everyone his fellow or everyone his brother saying, know the Lord. For all shall know Me, from the least of them to the greatest, for I will be merciful toward their iniquities, and I will remember their sins no more" (Hebrews 8:8-12).

The Old Testament examples of the family covenant are many: Noah, Joshua, Abraham, Moses, Isaac, Jacob and David. God saved Noah and his whole household from the flood even though Noah himself seems to have been the only really righteous person. Joshua said, "As for me and my house, we will serve the Lord." He didn't even bother to put the matter to a vote! In the Old Testament God often calls Himself "the God of Abraham, Isaac and Jacob." Many times He blesses "for His servant David's sake." He said, "I will make an everlasting covenant with the house of David."

Sometimes the family covenant is also used in a negative sense. In the Old Testament, Korah and Aachan are examples of this. The judgment of God, like the blessings of God, included families and generations. We relate to God not only as individuals but also in community since the Church is a body. In counseling I have often been amazed at the way that both blessing and judgment run in family patterns.

In praying the family covenant, two or more members of a family should agree perfectly (Matthew 18:19-20) and then join with an intercessor or intercessory group. Many times the person being prayed for cannot be approached in any other way and may be totally unaware that he is being prayed for at all. This is not an invasion of personal freedom but a way of keeping the devil, the world and the flesh from mobilizing their defenses against the Spirit.

The most common concern in families is not physical or emotional health but spiritual condition. When the church is being renewed, it is rare for any two people in a family to be in exactly the same stage of spiritual growth. There may be a whole gamut of reactions to the Word in the same family. Sometimes marriages which have not been primarily based in Christ will be torn apart and rebuilt when the Spirit comes.

First Corinthians 7:14 makes a strong case for the spiritual family covenant, "For the unbelieving husband is consecrated through his wife. And the unbelieving wife is consecrated through her husband. Otherwise your children would be unclean but as it is they are holy." Here also may be an answer for the nagging question of what happens to unbaptized infants when they die.

All of this does not mean that we can be saved by the faith of others but that we have a spiritual right and a strong obligation to make intercession for the salvation of members of our families. God hears these prayers in a special way. We may not see the results right away but that makes little difference in the perspective of eternity.

The Lord once burdened George Muller to pray for conversion of six of his friends. Two were converted almost immediately, two others after a period of time. Although he prayed for the last two on his knees with tears three times a day for forty-four years, they remained unconverted at the time of his death. They were brought to the Lord twelve years after Pastor Muller died!

The family covenant includes the healing of relationships. Very often the members of a family do not know or will not believe that their relationships need healing. It is hardest to forgive those closest to us. Husbands, wives and children hoard up hurts like a miser hoards gold. In the secret chambers of self they gloat over these slights, real or imagined.

Children may remain angry or resentful towards their parents years after the parents have died. This unforgiveness subtly poisons the streams of healing and of prayer.

Since I have little time for marriage counseling, I minister "marriage healing" instead. This consists of a short interview with the couple, sometimes together and sometimes alone. Usually one or the other of the marriage partners has made an initial contact.

When the picture of the marriage is somewhat in focus, we move from my office to the altar of the church. Often this has been preceded by private confession and absolution in the case of secret marital infidelity. If they do not desire private confession, I ask them to confess to God and each other before His altar. Then I ask them to join hands and make new marriage vows to each other. Then I lay a hand on each hand and ask that God would heal and seal the marriage with His Spirit.

Here is a prayer for the healing of a marriage: "Lord, we claim Your marriage covenant in Ephesians 5:21-33. If this marriage has been built on any other foundations, tear them out and rebuild it. It takes two to make a church. Make this marriage a basic and living cell of Your body. Let the partners agree together perfectly so that You can answer them in heaven.

"Bind them together with Your love so that, as heirs together of the grace of life, their prayers may not be hindered. Show them that marriage may sometimes be a crucifixion because the church also crucifies You. Heal their relationship beginning at the deepest level of forgotten resentments and unforgiveness. Bring all past hurts and bitterness into the light and cleansing power of Your presence.

"If they were once married by custom and tradition only, remarry them right now in the Spirit. If their marriage has lost that first love, renew this through prayer and the laying on of hands. Bind heart to heart and spirit to spirit in the most beautiful earthly communion that we mortals are capable of.

"In the name of Him who sanctified and confirmed marriage by His presence at the wedding at Cana. Amen."

The first thing that usually happens in the family covenant prayer is discernment. Hidden resentments, guilt, anger and jealousy begin to surface. As we continue to pray together once or even twice a week, the process of healing and reconciliation begins. Physical, emotional and spiritual healings take place in the entire family. The original incentive for prayer may have been the physical illness of a family member, but in this covenant intercession they always receive exceeding abundantly more than they could ask or imagine.

Sometimes there are intimate physical and emotional problems in the marriage. If both partners are frank and highly motivated, the results of marriage healing can be dramatic and even spectacular. A fine young Christian couple had been seeing doctors, psychiatrists and counselors for two and one-half years without results. There was an unexplainable failure in the physical relationship.

"It is with a deep sense of thanksgiving to God that I write to you," the husband wrote. "First of all I felt God's healing power beginning to work that evening during the beautiful prayer you had for me and my wife. The problem we shared with you just disappeared after two and one-half years of total frustration. . . . Yes, the Lord does heal. I'm so very, very grateful to Him. . . . "

The wife wrote on the back of her husband's letter: "I feel I have to add a word too! Never have I praised God so much as I have the past week. I can't even begin to describe the beauty of the healing He has given our marriage. He has not only healed the physical side of it, but I know He has touched the very depths of our relationship to each other and to Him. Your prayer left nothing untouched. So I know as a result we will continue to discover the many blessings He has in store for us."

At this writing a book on the family covenant is on the drawing board. Tapes are already available through the Trinity Lutheran Church tape ministry. Bible passages to consider are: Acts 11:14, and 16:31; 1 Peter 3:7; 1 Corinthians 7:14; John 19:26-27; Ephesians 5:29-32. Old Testament passages include 2 Chronicles 30:19-20; 1 Samuel 1:26-28; Exodus 2:24, and 3:6; II Kings 20:5-6; Psalms 105:9-10 and 32:11-12; Genesis 17:18-20 and 27:12-13; Exodus 20:5-6 and 6:2-4.

The question continually haunts us, *why are some healed and not others*? I have seen thousands healed and tens of thousands apparently not healed. Why are some prayers answered and not others? Why is the prayer of Elijah answered and much smaller prayers seemingly ignored? Much human speculation and sheer nonsense has been written about this. Perhaps the best available answer is that we honestly do not know. We see in a mirror dimly; we know in part and we prophesy in part. Some day we shall know as we are known.

Of some things we can be fairly certain, even now. Those who go to the Lord in faith and obedience never return empty-handed. There are no failures in prayer. We may not get what we want just when we want it and in the way we want, but we always receive abundantly more than we can ask, think or imagine. We fear to pray or be prayed for because we dread the possibility of God's rejection. If He doesn't answer immediately, that means that He doesn't love me or I don't really believe or perhaps I'm being punished for some secret sin.

In June of 1974 I prayed for about a hundred people in a service. Perhaps 25 percent were healed or helped and the rest apparently were not. The next morning the question was raised, "What about the faith and feelings of those who weren't healed? Isn't it possible that great harm was done to them?"

I answered with another question, "Suppose I had been afraid to pray for the sick last night because I knew they would not all be healed. Or suppose those who came forward would have been afraid to come because they might not be healed. What would have happened to the twenty-five?

"After all, we are all members of one body. If one is healed we are all healed. If one is sick we are all sick. We rejoice and weep with those who weep. We ought to praise the Lord for every single person who is healed just as the angels in heaven rejoice over every lost sinner who repents."

One thing is certain, the Lord wants us to keep in touch. The one who comes forward for physical healing is like a patient on the operating table. While the surgeons have him opened they try to repair everything that is wrong. While the Lord has us on our knees and before His throne He tries to heal the spirit, the emotions and the relationships as well.

8

FAITH

Lord, increase our faith. Teach us to understand that faith is God's gift to the believer. Remove all doubt and give us the faith of a child.

Holy Spirit of God, we know that we cannot believe by our own reason or strength. Therefore, come with Your divine inspiration, call us by the Gospel and enlighten us with Your gifts. May we always claim the highest willingness of God and know that He is able to give us abundantly more than we can ask, think or imagine.

Jesus, as You spoke to the woman from Tyre and Sidon, so speak to us, "Great is your faith, be it unto you as you have desired." Do not let us be afraid of Your silence or rejection, but keep on asking until You answer.

Heavenly Father, as Jacob wrestled with You in prayer through the night, so may we give all of our strength and attention to this mighty encounter.

Jesus, show us how to pray the prayer of faith, and thank and praise You in advance for what You are going to do. O Holy Spirit, make us to abide in the Word and in constant communion with God so that our faith may be living and powerful.

In the name of Him
Who opened the new and
living way to the Father, Jesus.

Faith is the only condition the Bible gives for anything that God offers. Yet only three passages in the entire Bible tell what faith is. "Now faith is the assurance of things hoped for, the conviction of things not seen. For by it the men of old gained approval. By faith we understand that the worlds were prepared by the Word of God, so that what is seen was not made out of things which are visible" (Hebrews 11:1-3).

Faith is the actualizer of the invisible world. Our sight, hearing, touch, taste and smell bring the visible world of nature to us. Faith is the sense and the gift of God that makes the invisible real to us. It is also the way that we receive divine approval and understand that the ultimate reality is spirit.

Faith is a perception of those transcendent truths which cannot be apprehended in any other way. Knowledge, feeling and even experience are not Biblical faith. It is an entity all of its own that serves a totally unique function. It links the finite with the infinite, the conditioned with the unconditioned. It is also the final key to the mystery of intercession.

110

The opposite of faith is not unbelief or doubt but fear. The fruits of true faith are not pure doctrine but obedience and love. However, obedience must often precede faith. When Jesus met someone He frequently issued a command, "Sell all you have," "Follow Me," "Stretch forth your hand," etc. "By this My Father is glorified that you bear much fruit, and so prove to be My disciples. As the Father has loved Me so have I loved you: abide in My love. If you keep My commandments you will abide in My love just as I have kept My Father's commandments and abide in His love" (John 15:8-10).

Faith is also a natural human quality. It is that which Dr. Norman Vincent Peale calls "positive thinking" and Christian Science uses for "faith healing." Life itself is faith. You couldn't cross a street, ride a bus or fly in a plane without it.

Faith is imagination, since man is highly suggestible. The most frequently used medication is the placebo or sugar pill. Double blind experiments have also proven that the sugar pill can be the most powerful pain killer of all. Dr. Jerome Frank, who teaches psychiatry in John Hopkins Medical School, says that if he were in private practice he would prescribe faith for one-third of his patients.

Dr. Nolen of Minneapolis sharply criticized the late Kathryn Kuhlman in magazine articles and in at least one book. He said that most of her so-called cures were based upon suggestion. Some of what he said is undoubtedly true but he is guilty of sloppy research and tremendous inconsistency. What he says of Kathryn Kuhlman's healings could also be said about every patient who leaves his office.

Since it is the best medicine he has, the doctor ought always to come down on the side of faith, no matter what he believes personally.

111

Barbara is a practicing Roman Catholic. After Betty Ford and "Happy" Rockefeller had breast surgery, almost every American woman began to examine her breasts. Barbara found a number of lumps. She went to her doctor and made an appointment for a biopsy on the following Wednesday. On the Friday night before, she came to our healing service and was prayed for. When she got home at eleven that night, the lumps had all disappeared without a trace.

On Wednesday she kept her appointment with the doctor but there wasn't anything to do a biopsy on. He seemed disappointed and even angry. Barbara told him what had happened.

He said, "They'll come back; they'll come back; don't worry." But they didn't and he seems terribly upset about the whole thing.

Myra is a beautiful black school teacher. She developed a hoarseness in her voice and went to see her doctor when it persisted. He found two tumors in her throat. The biopsy showed malignancy. The doctor told her to take a trip south to visit her relatives and come in on a certain day for surgery.

On the way south she stopped by to be prayed for. Sometime during the trip the hoarseness and the pain went away. But on the appointed day she checked into the hospital for an operation and a ten-day stay. Her husband settled down in the waiting room for a day-long vigil.

The surgeons were gowned and masked and the operating rooms staff were all prepared. But after only thirty minutes Myra reappeared, carrying her bag and wreathed in smiles. Her doctor followed her looking a little embarrassed.

"Let's go home," she said to her husband.

"What's the matter, did they have to postpone the operation?" he asked somewhat puzzled.

"No, the tumors were gone."

"What do you mean gone?"

"Not a trace of them to be found," Myra announced, looking back meaningfully at the doctor.

"Doctor, do you mean to stand there and tell me that we went to all this expense and worry for tumors that didn't even exist? Just what were you and that other doctor planning to cut out?" Ben said angrily.

"I don't understand it," the doctor said. "It must have been the country air."

"Do you mean to stand there and tell me that country air removes tumors from the throat? Doctor, I'm not a medical man but I'm no fool."

"Well, I just don't understand it, but I'll examine her some more," the doctor concluded lamely. He seemed anxious to get the whole thing over with. By now the entire surgical staff was standing in the background watching and wondering.

The doctor had Myra come back every week free of charge. He would stare into her throat, shake his head and mutter, "I don't understand it but they'll be back." Saying that somehow seemed to make him feel better.

After three months of this, I said to Myra, "Stop going to that man. Before you know it he's going to talk those tumors back in. He doesn't know it but he's shooting down his own medicine." Myra stopped going.

Natural faith and gift faith overlap. Everything that God gives is at one and the same time gift response. He freely and fully gives all things and then expects our full and free response to these gifts. Many times when Jesus healed He said, "Thy faith hath made thee whole." Somehow faith was a part of the healing package and yet the response remained totally free. Faith is God's gift to the believer.

Great faith is simply that inability to doubt. If we could say to a mountain, "Be removed into the sea" and then not doubt in any part of one's being, it would happen. But we cannot possibly say a ridiculous thing like that without doubting a little.

The faith of a child illustrates this clearly. A Roman Catholic woman had five children with severe dyslexia (learning disabilities). She also worked in a school for handicapped children. Frequently she brought children to be prayed for.

I would take them into the office and ask if they knew Jesus personally. If they said yes, then I would say, "Now do you really believe He is going to heal you?"

"Yes, Pastor."

"Do you doubt even one little bit?"

"No, Pastor."

They didn't doubt because they were too naive. They simply didn't know how to doubt or to pretend. Many were healed. Sometimes measured reading and math levels went up three years in one night. Report cards that had listed D's and F's before, now showed A's and B's. Then they would proudly bring them to the altar and praise the Lord for His healing power.

During one of the Minneapolis conferences a little boy came up with the first joint of his little finger cut off.

"If you pray for it, it will grow back," he more or less announced to me.

"Son, you've really thrown me a curve this time. Would you mind coming back this afternoon? I need some time to think about it."

I had half hoped he wouldn't, but he did come back with his parents. His face and faith were both shining.

"Son, do you really believe that finger joint will grow back if I pray? You don't have a bit of doubt in your mind?"

I was stalling for time. I turned to the parents. "Do you believe too?"

114

"Yes, Pastor, we believe."

Lord, what do I do now, because you know I don't believe? I prayed silently.

The answer came immediately, *You've lengthened hundreds of legs. Have you even thought of trying to lengthen a finger?*

Praise the Lord! I grasped the finger and began to pray. Suddenly both little fingers were exactly the same length. Gradually a new nail and new skin began to grow over the restored joint. Oh, for the faith of a child!

Sometimes faith is experience with God. In the Old Testament God always calls Israel's attention to the mighty works He has done for them in the past as a basis for faith and trust for the uncertain and unknown future. The Exodus from Egypt and the parting of the Red Sea are often used in this way.

One type of healing has always worked for me and that is leg lengthening. Perhaps it always works because I always believe it will. Many attempts have been made to explain this in some rational way but often the lengthening is as much as three inches. Sometimes there have been exact medical measurements made before and after the prayer.

This principle of faith has been extended to arm and even nose lengthening and also back straightening. It seems that if we really expect the Lord to do something, He will do it. The experience of faith keeps building up to greater and greater heights.

God has promised to supply all our needs. He can do this in any way He sees fit. In Indonesia where wine is very difficult to obtain He turns water into wine at the consecration of the communion elements. In the same way God tends to heal most frequently those things for which medicine has not yet found an answer.

The disease that has been healed most often by

prayer in our service is arthritis. Medicine has no answer for this all too common condition except aspirin and cortisone. By the same token I have never seen tonsils taken out by prayer. I've heard of teeth being filled but have never prayed for it.

Faith Is Relationship

"Abide in Me and I in you. As the branch cannot bear fruit by itself, unless it abides in the vine, neither can you unless you abide in Me. I am the vine, you are the branches. He who abides in Me and I in him, he it is that bears much fruit, for apart from Me you can do nothing" (John 15:4-5). Without this relationship it is impossible to please God no matter how good you are (Hebrews 11:6).

Because faith is relationship it needs to be fed in order to live. Because it is relationship to a living vine it needs to bear fruit. "Every branch of mine that bears no fruit, he takes away, and every branch that does bear fruit he prunes, that it may bear more fruit (John 15:2).

In my hospital chaplaincies there were frequent encounters with patients who said, "Chaplain, I haven't been to church or (mass) in thirty years but I still believe; I haven't lost my faith."

"I've got news for you. You may still believe certain religious truths but your faith has long since starved to death. It's only a fossil memory," I would usually reply.

"What do you mean by that, Chaplain?"

"What happens to a relationship that isn't fed? Suppose you would leave your wife for thirty years. What would happen to your marriage? Or suppose you had a good friend but didn't visit, call or write him for thirty years. What would happen to your friendship?"

"Oh, I think I get your point, Chaplain. As soon as I get out of the hospital I'm going to go back to church. You can bet on that."

116

But they seldom did. Only God can raise the dead.

Because faith is relationship, little children can also have it. A day-old baby can have a real relationship with its mother and its heavenly Father. The Church will probably never resolve the issue of infant vs. believers' baptism because it can never get out of the medieval swamp of rational faith. The moanings and groanings of the Spirit give us a hint that much of faith occurs at a subliminal level.

Since faith is a living relationship it is not an on-again-off-again kind of thing. The story is told of a Scotch family who put up with a butter-fingered maid for several years. She kept breaking things and they warned her again and again. When she broke a piece of expensive crystal, they regretfully fired her.

Soon afterwards a son and heir was born into the household. As soon as he was old enough to be mobile he began to explore. One day he found a tempting piece of cloth to pull on. He pulled and he tugged until the whole set of crystal on the tablecloth came crashing down on the floor. The parents were very, very upset but they did not fire the baby.

Rationalists love to argue religion. When I was a chaplain intern at City Hospital in Baltimore, patients would often greet me by saying abruptly, "Chaplain, I'm an atheist."

"Congratulations! It takes a lot of faith to be an atheist."

"What do you mean by that? Sit down I want to talk to you."

Comfortably seated I would begin, "First of all, it takes courage not to believe in any absolute. Secondly, it must be very hard to live without a supreme value. Finally, it takes tremendous credulity to believe that Michaelangelo's frescoes and Handel's *Messiah* come from a tiny speck of solar dust."

A little groggy, they would usually say, "Well, if you

can't believe, you can't believe. You wouldn't want me to be a hypocrite, would you? I've tried but there are just too many things I can't swallow. What do you suggest, Chaplain?"

Several years later I ran across Pascal's famous wager. It goes something like this: "Live as if God did exist and everything He says in His Word is literally true. Then if at the end of life you discover that it was all a pack of lies, you haven't lost a thing. You have lived as perfect a human life as could be lived on this earth. But if you bet against God and lose, you have lost everything in this life and the life to come."

"If any of you lacks wisdom, let him ask God, who gives to all men generously and without reproaching and it will be given him. But let him ask in faith with no doubting, for he who doubts is like a wave of the sea that is driven and tossed by the wind. For that person must not suppose that a double-minded man, unstable in all his ways, will receive anything from the Lord" (James 1:5-8).

The prayer of the double-minded man says "yes" and "no" to God at the same time. God always hears and answers the "no." The man says with his lips, "I want to be healed," and with his heart, "I can't be healed." God hears and answers the heart. Sometimes like Augustine we put a postscript on our prayers. Augustine prayed, "Lord, make me pure but not just yet; Lord, cleanse me from every sin but one." The postscript became the prayer.

If the double-minded man gets nothing from the Lord, the man who returns to thank and praise God for His answer gets the whole package. This is the story of the tenth leper, the Samaritan. The nine lepers with him received physical healing and nothing more. The tenth leper who returned to give thanks and praise to God received total healing. Faith includes not just

118

asking and receiving but thanksgiving and praise as well.

Luther says in his explanation to the last article in the Apostles' Creed, "I believe that I cannot believe." ("I believe that I cannot by my own reason or strength believe in Jesus Christ, my Lord, or come to Him, but the Holy Spirit has called me by the Gospel and enlightened me with His gifts.") Saving faith is gift-response. Only supernatural faith is a gift of the Spirit (1 Corinthians 12:9).

In Romans, chapters 3 and 4, we see that faith is the only way of receiving God's righteousness, salvation and eternal life. In the Old Testament it was a response to God's mighty acts, especially the Exodus from Egypt. In the New Testament it is a response to the Gospel, especially the resurrection. In Galatians 3, faith is the way of receiving all the promises of God. Faith is the only condition in the Bible for receiving anything from God. First comes faith and then comes experience. After the resurrection Jesus showed Himself only to those who had believed in Him before His death. "We walk by faith and not by sight" (2 Corinthians 5:7).

Hebrews 11 shows how the great Old Testament heroes of the faith surrendered themselves totally to the promises of God. This is more than just believing; it is obedience. We pray and believe, not simply to get something we want but because God has commanded it. The prayer of faith is a command as well as a promise. In Matthew 7:7 and Luke 11:9 faith is largely a matter of obedience. "Ask, seek, knock."

James 2 describes the relationship between faith and works. Faith cannot be expanded by human works. Works are only a sign that faith is real. The only thing we can do is allow the total and radical surrender of our wills to God's grace. The surrender of faith makes a man authentic and complete. Works are never completed. Faith is the only way of life for one who has been crucified with Christ. Faith is not merely something in which we stand but also walk.

We live in the tension between the "now" and the "not yet." Only faith can bridge the gap and claim all the blessings and promises of God now. We walk in the tension of flesh and spirit, visible and invisible, pain and hope. In the struggle, only faith can gain the victory. In the dark mysteries of life's great paradoxes, faith alone can light the way to the loving heart of God. It is a deliberate turning away from works, world and men, toward the invisible God. Through faith our real lives are "hid with Christ in God" (Colossians 3:1-4).

Finally, faith is neither doctrine nor believing; it is relationship. It is a living relationship with the Father through the Spirit of Christ. This relationship must be nourished by Word, sacrament and worship. Man cannot live by bread alone. The Word is man's food between his baptism and his resurrection.

Any relationship, friendship, family, business that is not continually fed will die. As relationship, faith is also growth. Whenever a man, animal or plant stops growing, it automatically begins to die. We cannot stay on some comfortable plateau with God. We are to grow up to the stature and image of Jesus Christ. That is a long way to go, but we must be growing if true intercession is our goal.

9

INTERCESSION
FROM THE CROSS

Jesus, we thank You for Your intercessions from the cross. May we use them as patterns for our own prayer lives. Your blood contained the very life of God which is still crying out for us from the soil of Golgotha.

Father, as You forgave the murderers of Your beloved Son, teach us to forgive our enemies. As He cried out to You in His human need, "I thirst," so may we bring every need to You.

Jesus, hear every cry for salvation, as You heard that of the dying thief on the cross. When we cry out in despair, "My God, my God, why hast Thou forsaken me," let us hear that answering echo in the darkness.

Jesus, we pray the family covenant for all our loved ones through Your love for Your mother even as You were dying on the cross. Holy Spirit, bring the finished work of Jesus into our lives so that we may not try to redeem or sanctify ourselves. Show us that we cannot atone for our own sins or make ourselves worthy to come into Your presence and claim Your gifts.

Jesus, You said, "Father, into Thy hands I commend My Spirit." So may we surrender every area of life and all of ourselves to the Father's temporal and eternal care. Father, Son and Holy Spirit, accept the sacrifice of our lives as a freewill offering. Amen.

The great intercessory prayer of Jesus, John 14-17, was made right before He went to the cross. The next day the prayer was sealed forever by His death. The "seven last words" from the cross are also seven intercessions which are directly plugged in to the power of the redemption. On the cross Jesus is interceding for us not only in words but in blood, sweat and tears. His very life is poured out in intercession for the transgressors.

The first intercession, "Father, forgive them for they know not what they do," is the most powerful. This is the very heart of our salvation. When we pray this prayer with Jesus, we use God's own weapons to overcome evil. This dying prayer of Stephen may have given the Apostle Paul to the church.

On Labor Day 1967, we were relaxing in the parsonage at 30 Jefferson Street in Brooklyn, New York. Holidays are rare in a pastor's schedule and quiet ones almost unknown. We knew better than to venture onto the streets and highways. Traffic to the beaches or out of town would be backed up for miles in and out. We thought about taking the subway to Manhattan but almost everything would be closed anyhow. So we decided to just relax as a family for a change.

Years later in Joppatowne, Maryland, I learned the trick of filing the phone under P, taking it off the hook and closing the cabinet door to drown out the indignant beeps. On this Labor Day the phone did not take a holiday. It began to ring urgently.

The voice on the other end sounded like panic in a Spanish accent.

"Riot—there's a riot! Richard is being beat up. They are arresting him! It's right across the street; I can see everything!"

I ran the two blocks over to Broadway. When I got there the riot squad had just left and the local precinct police had taken Richard away in handcuffs. Everybody in the block was excitedly chattering in English and Spanish. All I could make out was, "Blackie, stolen car, Richard, the police beat them and took them away."

Richard was a husky ex-sailor, ex-alcoholic, turned saint. He was a house painter who spent his spare time ministering to drunks and working with Boy Scouts. Many times he would go to the Bowery in Manhattan, pick up the unconscious "stiffs" and take them to some shelter. To the people on his block, young and old, black, white and brown, Richard was a twentieth century Saint Francis. He had been trying to keep the police from beating a small black Puerto Rican the day he was arrested.

I borrowed a car and with Ann, Richard's wife, went to the 79th Precinct in the Bedford Stuyvesant section of Brooklyn. When he recognized Ann, the desk sergeant became considerably less than cooperative. She had written several letters to the mayor complaining about two patrolmen shaking down pushcart peddlers. One of them had once asked her, "Do you know what happens to people who write to the mayor about the police?"

123

I asked for the captain. He wasn't in. A lieutenant came out and I told him what I had heard.

"Do you want to file a citizen's complaint?" he asked arrogantly.

"Yes, I certainly do, and I also want to know what you have done with Richard!"

At that very moment they were beating him upstairs, but the lieutenant lied and said, "They've already taken him down to headquarters at Schermerhorn Street."

We searched all day. It was one big, fat run-around. Seldom has a man in a clerical collar been told so many lies in one single day. Finally, at nine o'clock in the evening they brought Richard out into the courtroom on Schermerhorn Street in downtown Brooklyn.

When I saw him, it was like a dream: where had I seen this before? It was almost a passion play. The words *"ecce homo,"* (behold the man), burst forth from my lips. It was like Christ before Pilate!

On the way home Richard told his incredible story. He had been beaten at the 79th Precinct by several huge patrolmen. Every time they hit him Richard would say, "Father, forgive them for they know not what they do."

Once when they were beating Blackie, Richard threw his large body on top of the tiny black Puerto Rican to keep him from being killed. This time they beat Richard unconscious with night sticks. When he came to, a two-hundred-forty-pound patrolman was leering at him.

"Now you can tell your wife what happens to people who write to the mayor about the police!" the officer sneered with hate-filled eyes.

Through swollen lips and broken teeth, Richard managed to smile and say, "God loves you and I love you."

Later on Richard and I were invited to go on Fortune

Radio in New York and tell our story. As a result we were persecuted but extensive reforms were carried out in the entire New York City Police Department. I would like to believe that *Serpico* was made possible by Richard's prayer. When we pray, "Father, forgive," we plug directly into the infinite voltage of the cross.

The second intercession from the cross, "I thirst," establishes the true humanity of Jesus. He is our brother, tempted in all things like ourselves, yet without sin. Many times in counseling, the troubled person asks the counselor, "Do you really understand how I feel?"

Sometimes I say, "I think so but I can't be absolutely sure; however, I do know that God understands exactly how you feel because Christ went through the same thing."

The cross means that God not only identifies with our sin but also with all of our troubles. He who counts the hairs of our heads and watches the sparrows fall knows every worry, pain and fear. He knows us better than we know ourselves because He looks deep, deep inside at the most hidden pain and the cry of the heart.

Rehabilitation is often based upon identification. Only one alcoholic can understand another. That's the basic principle upon which A.A. is founded.

Old Bill had been a wino for forty years. At one time he was a policeman, but then his wife left him and he had been feeling sorry for himself ever since. Many times he came into my office weeping and asked for prayer. He would put his arms on my shoulders and sob heart-breaking, drunken sobs. Because he was so unsteady we both usually ended up on the floor.

Another favorite trick was to go to sleep on my doorbell at four in the morning. I talked to him, prayed with him, counseled and lectured till I ran completely out of patience. Nothing helped. I simply wasn't talking his language.

One Saturday I sat Bill on the couch in the waiting room and called for an A.A. veteran who had been sober for twenty-three years. I watched and listened. It was a miracle. In five minutes he got through to Bill and accomplished more than I had in months. He could talk Bill's language! Only one drunk can talk to another. Only one broken heart can speak to another broken heart.

Because Jesus had human needs like thirst, God understands our language. He knows exactly what the problem is and what to do about it. He is not sitting up in heaven on a cloud of glory telling us to hang on. He is standing right beside us in the depths, bearing and sharing all things.

The third intercession from the cross is, "Today shalt thou be with me in Paradise." The thief on the cross in his dying moments had said, "Lord, remember me when You come into Your kingdom." This is a request that God cannot refuse. He who calls upon the name of the Lord shall be saved (Romans 10:9-10).

The genuine, sincere prayer for salvation will always be answered. When we ask in penitent faith, "Lord, come into my heart," He always comes. It's so simple and yet so terribly difficult. There is nothing we have to do or can do. The thief on the cross was never baptized and had never communed. He may never have been inside a church, synagogue or temple in his entire life.

Paradise was opened on that day when Jesus died. According to some of the church fathers, when Jesus descended into Hell, the Old Testament believers were transferred from "Sheol" to "Paradise." Probably the first one to enter that newly opened realm was a life-long criminal, simply because he had prayed the prayer that God cannot refuse.

Whoever you are, whatever you may be, you can say to Jesus right now, "Lord, remember me." He cannot

126

refuse. This covenant is sealed in His own blood.

The fourth intercession from the cross is, "Son, behold thy mother; woman behold thy Son." This is the real basis for the family covenant. With the weight of the world's sins on his back, at the very brink of death, Jesus could still think of His mother. The family is important to God.

Mother is usually the first witness and the first preacher in our lives. From her we learn the first prayer and first hear the name of Jesus. God is love but that remains only an abstraction to a child until parents express love to him.

Simeon told Mary in the temple, while he was holding the baby Jesus in his arms, "And a sword shall pierce your own heart also." Once another Eve had stood before another tree and brought sin and death into the world through her disobedience. Now the second Eve was standing beneath the tree of the cross, offering up the fruit of her body for the sin of her sister.

For this reason women pay the greatest price for men's violence and cruelty. Again and again, they are called to offer up their sons to the cruel god of war. For this reason also, mother-love is most like God's love. A mother will accompany her son all the way to the gallows weeping, "I don't care what he did, he's still my son."

Because mothers are the first missionaries and the greatest martyrs, they also are the best intercessors for the family covenant. A mother is almost always willing to die for her child, and many are even willing to go to hell for them. David is an example of a parent-intercessor. When Absalom was killed and damned, David cried, "Oh, Absalom, my son, my son, would to God that I had died for thee" (II Samuel 18:33).

The family covenant is a powerful prayer because Jesus prayed it from the cross. It is a part of God's old and new covenant. He says to all parents and children who seek the salvation of a loved one, "Pray for thy mother; mother, pray for thy son."

The fifth intercession from the cross is, "My God, my God, why hast thou forsaken me?" When Jesus died the sun hid its face. The earth quaked. The dead were raised. The veil of the temple was torn apart. Men shouted and cursed. Horses neighed. Soldiers gambled. But God was silent. You could have heard a pin drop from heaven. At that moment Jesus felt completely abandoned by God and men.

We can certainly understand that feeling. When we cry out alone in the darkness, there is an answering echo from the cross. When we reach out from the depths of despair, there is a hand with a nail hole in it.

Despair is where we find God. He is not in the safe and secure place, but on the margins and in the depths.

Loneliness is one of the greatest human burdens. On an empty street in a St. Louis ghetto there once was an abandoned building. The windows were broken and the walls were crumbling. On that wrecked and empty building a huge, unpainted sign flapped in the wind. Its faded letters read, "Lonely Hearts Club." The scene is etched on my memory. It is filled with all the loneliness of hell.

But we need never be lonely or alone. He who felt abandoned on the cross is always with us. When we go Indian file through birth and death and operating rooms, He is always there beside us. He goes with us where no human can follow. Even when we forget Him, He does not forget us. Because He once cried out in the agony of despair, "My God, my God, why hast Thou forsaken me?" we never have to be forsaken.

The sixth intercession from the cross is, "It is finished." With these words the sacrificial system of the Old Testament comes to an abrupt end. There is now no longer any sacrifice for sin. We cannot offer up our own happiness, health or peace of mind as atonement for our sin (Hebrews 10:1-18).

When I was chaplain of Greenpoint Hospital in Brooklyn, New York, I ministered to many patients of Roman Catholic background. Often they would say, "Chaplain, I've been sick all my life, but God will reward me some day for all of this suffering. He won't punish me for my sins because I've been through so much already."

"Do you believe you can atone for your own sin by suffering?" I would ask.

"Yes, isn't that the way Christ paid for our sins?"

"But He said, 'It is finished.' God cannot accept your suffering as atonement because there is only one mediator between God and man— Christ Jesus" (I Timothy 2:5).

I don't know whether I ever really got my point across. We are so deeply programed to believe that God enjoys suffering for suffering's sake. That is why so many are chronically ill and unhappy. Man would rather be his own judge and jury than trust the mercy of God.

The seventh intercession from the cross is, "Father into Thy hand I commend my Spirit." This is the prayer of surrender. This is the intercession which says, "Let go and let God."

This is the hardest intercession of all. It's so hard for us to let go of anything. It's so hard to say, "Father, into Thy hands I commend my life, my failure," or "Father, into Thy hands I commend my family, my friends and my enemies." Can we ever really say, "Father, into Thy hands I commend all my resentment and hurt, my worry and my anger"?

Until we let go and place our Isaacs on the altar, God won't take over. As long as we try to deal with

129

our enemy, God won't touch him. He says, "Good luck but you are going to get clobbered." As long as we try to solve our own problems alone, God won't interfere.

We need to let go of ourselves, of things and of people. If we cannot let go of things, they become idols and stand between us and God. If we cannot let go of people, neither we nor they can be free and whole.

Several years ago I was ministering to a dying man in a Baltimore hospital. He was in intensive care in great pain. He was ready to go and wanted to go. But he couldn't die because his family wouldn't let him go. Finally, I walked outside and said to his wife, "You've just got to let him go so that he can die in peace." After a great struggle and many tears, she agreed, and he went joyfully to meet his Lord.

It's very difficult for parents to let go of children and often for children to let go of parents. The prayer, "Father, into Thy hands I commend my Spirit," is a freeing prayer. It sets us free to be holy, to love, to live and to die in peace and security. It makes us slaves of God so that we can be free indeed (John 8:31-36). Only the free are able to love and God is love. We cannot relate to Him outside of the freedom of faith. At one and the same moment we can be totally free and completely controlled by God. Freedom means the ability to fulfill our purpose. We were made for God and we cannot rest until we rest in Him, because Jesus was the only really free man who has ever lived.

10

INTERCESSION
AND THE CHURCH

Jesus, let us see You in Your body, the Church. You hide Your life in Your Word; let that Word become flesh in our lives.

Father, we thank You for the baptism which brings us into Your kingdom and for Holy Communion through which we partake of You.

Jesus, may our hearts burn within us as we recognize You in the breaking of the bread. Let all the seven thousand promises of the Bible be ours. In the real presence of Holy Communion, may we claim all three hundred of Jesus' words and all of His ministries.

Heal and unite Your Church, Lord, so that it may be able to pray for the healing of the nations. Renew Your Church, beginning with me, and hasten to ready the bride for Your coming.

Jesus, let the oil of healing and blessing run down from You, the Head, into every member of Your body. Amen.

Our age is not only secular but also sectarian. There is no end to the printing of books and the proliferation of sects. The Church and its liturgy are reinvented every day. It's almost like reinventing the wheel or rediscovering fire.

But the Church has a historical dimension which neither reformers nor renewers can ignore. We are the heirs of a costly, blood-bought faith. We are surrounded by a great cloud of witnesses (Hebrews 12:1).

Warts and all, the Church is the bride of Christ. She may be a bit old and wrinkled but she is the Lord's Body (1 Corinthians 2) and He loves her (Ephesians 5). The renewal which is now taking place is both a corrective and a preparation for the great wedding feast.

Because the Church has not always been obedient and because she has neglected some of the Lord's commands, the Spirit often has been forced to work outside the Church. Throughout the history of the Church there has been a tension between Spirit and structure. Up until now it appears that the structure has won. This time the Spirit is going to win.

Because of the struggle between Spirit and structure, many renewal movements have become anti-institutional. They are suspicious of creeds and liturgy. Formal or written prayers are almost blasphemy to most sectarians. Man is an institutional as well as a personal being. The only substitute for good structure is bad.

Often we end up with an elaborately structured "non-structure" or a highly ritualistic "non-ritual."

Spontaneity becomes rote and anti-tradition turns into fixed tradition. This is the "foolish Galatians" syndrome. The Gospel becomes a new law and the Spirit another pope. Those expelled from the structure become more rigid than the institution which cast them out. The Pilgrims came to this country to escape intolerance and they, in turn, became more intolerant than their former persecutors.

Healing miracles and the gifts of the Spirit have somehow become associated with circus tents and magic prayer cloths. The moment a person becomes spiritually renewed, the cry goes up, "Come out from among them!" This is how the Assemblies of God started and grew. Those who came out or were thrown out joined its fellowship. David du Plessis, "Mr. Pentecost," said that until 1948 he believed that the Lord was saying, "Come out." Since 1948, however, the Lord has been saying to him, "Go back. Don't run away; stay and pray."

God hides His life in His Word. The parable of the rich man and Lazarus shows that our eternal destiny is decided by our belief or unbelief of the Word. The Word of God is creative; it never returns void.

It is relevant for every situation in life. It's in the joy of a wedding and the tears of a funeral. By a word God spoke the worlds into existence. The Word pronounces the final Amen of history. We first heard the Word at baptism, in the cradle, in Sunday School and in our mother's prayers. It spans the creation and all of human life. It blesses the poor and the rich meal. Heaven and earth shall pass away, but the Word will not pass away.

The most popular versions of the Bible today are paraphrases. A best-selling paraphrase often bears little or no resemblance to the original text. It is a commentary reflecting the author's own political and theological views. Yet most Bible readers do not even know what the word *paraphrase* means. Again and again Christians come to me and ask, "Pastor, what does this word *paraphrase* stand for?"

Much of the Bible is written in a form of shorthand. For instance, the creation of the cosmos, all the stars, is described in one Hebrew word. Genesis 1:16, "He made the stars also," is one word, *kokavim,* in the original. The beatitudes in the Sermon on the Mount are also a form of shorthand. They can be properly understood only by a thorough study of the Greek and Hebrew background of the translations. If we really believe that the Word of God is infallible, then we will want it translated as accurately as possible.

Some of the most popular religious best sellers today fall into the category of Biblical science fiction. As has been pointed out many times, there is little real Biblical evidence for a "pretribulation rapture." There is also no evidence in the history of dogma that the doctrines of the "rapture" and of the "seven dispensations" appeared before the year 1830. Both have been traced to the ecstatic utterances of a Scotswoman named Margaret McDonald (*The Incredible Cover-up* by Dave MacPherson, Logos).

Word, sacrament and Church belong together. Here God wants to bless, heal and renew. The gifts of the Spirit belong right in the center of the Church and its altar, not on the fringes. By "signs following," God wants to confirm not tents and miracle cloths, but the Gospel and the Church.

Intercession also belongs right in the heart of the Church. This is Christ's Body linked together by His own life. The oil of anointing flows down from the head into all the members. The Church may seem dead at times, but she functions as a school mistress to hold God's people in place until the Spirit comes.

The "Spiritual Lone Rangers" flare up and flare out. If they prosper it is often to fall into grievous error and mislead the flock. During the time that I was pastor in Brooklyn, over a dozen storefronts on the block flared up and flamed out. The church went through many cycles but it held the saints in place until God moved.

Many historical churches believe in the "Real Presence" in Holy Communion. This goes all the way back to the Emmaus disciples who recognized the Lord in the breaking of the bread (Luke 24:30-32). The "Real Presence" means the whole presence of Jesus.

In Holy Communion we can receive not only the forgiveness of sins but also all seven thousand Bible promises. The Christ who becomes incarnate in His broken body and shed blood offers us here all His blessings and ministries. You can be healed, delivered and filled with the Spirit in Holy Communion! Thousands have given testimony to this truth.

Holy Communion is one of the few really objective things we do in the church. Here is God's sovereign "giveness." Nothing we do here is highly colored by our own subjectivity. How can you tell whether you are being moved by the emotions or Spirit? How can we be sure that God is really speaking? We can receive the sacrament for blessing or condemnation, but all of our thinking and doctrines cannot change its essential nature.

Intercession is a function of the Church—a form of "body ministry" in which all can participate silently or vocally. Here Spirit, Word and ministry are confirmed and linked together. God does not see us praying alone with all our faults and doubts. He sees Christ kneeling in the form of His Body, the Church.

The heavenly Father can deny nothing to His beloved Son. Praying in the name of Jesus means going through the Head of the Body straight to the Father's throne by means of that new and living way created by the cross of our Lord (Hebrews 10:19-25).

Conclusion

The great unfinished task of theology lies in the area of eschatology, or the "last things." Some large church bodies have painted themselves into a corner through Biblical science fiction. Others have left the issue pretty much open, and it has turned into a happy hunting ground for sects and fanatics.

The Old Testament seems to direct our attention primarily toward Israel and the Mideast. The barren, rocky, postage-stamp land of Palestine certainly has a special place in human destiny. The Crusades, with their strange combination of piety and piracy, set the stage for 1948. They finally lost the land but they built walls and monasteries which still stand. The 1967 war was like Gideon repeated, only with tanks and rockets. It was the most recent "Holy War."

The New Testament, on the other hand, seems to focus its eschatology more on nature and the Church. The great high priestly prayer, John 14-17, emphasizes the unity of the Church. "Father, I pray that they may be one as You and I are one" (John 17). Christ's prayer must be answered in history since the church is historical (1 Corinthians 3:8-13).

The enemy knows this well. He also knows that when Christ comes again, his time will be up forever. For this reason he fights hardest against church renewal and unity. He is most afraid of the sacrament of unity—Holy Communion.

The thing that all renewed Christians have in common is not tongues or doctrine but ecumenicity. Even the most conservative are almost automatically ecumenical. This characteristic more than anything else brings them into conflict with their separatistic denominations.

God, where are You taking us? Is all this fuss about the gifts of the Spirit merely a corrective to the heresy of omission or are we really approaching the end? It could be either one or both. One thing is certain, we are in a period of rapidly accelerating transition.

Will the Second Coming be a staged or a packaged event? Will there be a period of transition between history and non-history? Step right up, pay your money, and take your choice. We don't really know for sure what is coming, or when, or how, but we know Who is coming. If we don't know Him yet, then it's high time to get acquainted.

In view of the uncertain future of the Church and the world, the role of intercession becomes increasingly important. Abraham's intercession for Sodom is our model. "Lord, will You preserve the world for a little while longer if there are ten thousand righteous people still in it—or even nine? Lord, will You spare Your Church if there are still a thousand obedient saints—or less?"

Intercession might also go the other way. "Lord, will You come quickly and put an end to this mess if we witness and evangelize faithfully? Will You cleanse and unify Your church if we all join together in fervent intercession?" Either way, the golden key to the present and the future lies in the power of intercession. Now is the time for intercession. Very soon, it may be too late.

EPILOG

I know that the Spirit is trying to lead us into all truth. For a long time in our church there were physical healings; then came emotional healings, deliverance, deep healing and healing of relationships. After we broke through into intercession, the Spirit began to step on my heels.

First came the family covenant and then, after I came to Trinity Church in Joppa, the Lord opened up more and more of His plan. We started the discipleship course, and as this was being written and taught, a light began to break into the darkness.

Why was church renewal seemingly going sour in many places? Why didn't churches and prayer groups move or even get off the ground after years of praying? Why all the controversy and fear? Because we had failed to see the most elementary thing: sanctification is continuous growth (Hebrews 6:1-2).

Almost every denomination was getting hung up on one stage or another of this growth process and couldn't seem to break out. The historical churches were usually frozen at confirmation. Lutherans, theologically and spiritually, are frozen in eternal religious puberty. Baptists tend to get hung up on salvation. Because they often overstate it in their witness, any step beyond salvation becomes an anticlimax and a threat. Pentecostals seem to be petrified Baptists in the forest of spiritual gifts.

But there are other workings of the cross beyond salvation and baptism with the Holy Spirit. As I have already said, intercession goes out from oneself. This third working of the cross is where most renewal groups get hung up. Unless they are able to go out from themselves toward God and their fellow man, the other workings cannot follow.

All the steps are called "workings of the cross," because they are not additional works of grace but spring from our co-death and co-resurrection with Christ in water baptism and faith.

The fourth working of the cross is the realization that Christ is all in all. This is walking in the Spirit according to Romans 8. When we walk in the Spirit and not according to the law of sin and death, the supernatural becomes natural. We are already in the dimension of eternal life with both the judgment and resurrection behind us (Romans 8:1 and 11). 1 Thessalonians 4:13-18 presents this version of the "rapture."

When Jesus comes again, whether staged or packaged, millennial transition or none, the truly spiritual believers will meet the Lord "in the air," bypassing the judgment seat. When Christ becomes "all

140

in all," the times and seasons of prayer may be set aside. Life becomes a living, breathing prayer as every thought, word and deed passes in review before Him who is all in all.

The fifth working of the cross is "agape love" (1 Corinthians 13:4-13). Agape love is patient and kind; it is not arrogant and does not insist on its own way. Agape does not rejoice in wrong but in right. It bears all things, hopes all things, endures all things. The whole controversy in the church about authority and submission fades away like morning fog before the light of God's total self-giving love. There are three Greek words for love:

(1) *"The love that takes."* This is *eros* in Greek— love centered in the self. This love often exploits people for its own ends. This kind of love creates jealousy. In its most selfish form the "love that takes" is worse than hate.

(2) *"The love that gives and takes."* This is *filia* in Greek. It's bargain or exchange love. I love you because you love me. This kind of love is neutral and natural. It is neither bad nor good. Matthew 5:46-47 says that even Gentiles and tax collectors love with this kind of love.

(3) *"The love that only gives."* *Agape* love is subject and not object love. It is unconditional and even operates toward one's enemies (Matthew 5:43-45).

Once a spiritual man reaches this working of the cross, he also becomes aware of the horizontal dimension of the Gospel: "Thou shalt love thy neighbor as thyself." Christians often have been accused of a lack of social consciousness simply because they have not fully accepted God's "agape" and therefore cannot pass it on.

The sixth working of the cross is joyfully and fully doing the will of God. Jesus said in John 4:34, "My meat is to do the will of Him who sent me and to

141

accomplish His work." The will of God, for Jesus, was merely dessert or an appetizer. It was not a painful duty but "meat and drink," the very essence of His life, mission and being.

He was able to heal all who came to Him because He was perfectly in tune with this will. He was free to do the will of the Father even though it cost Him His followers, His security and even His life. This is the theme of the whole Gospel of John. Jesus' glory, His words, His mission, was to accomplish one thing: the will of the Father. For Him it was pure joy; for us it is often painful and burdensome.

We want to do our own thing and only bow before the superior power and authority of God. It's like saying, "God, You're bigger than I am, so You win. Your will is painful and tragic. Your will is the cross, but my will is security and blessing." God does not want to destroy our selfhood and make us either empty or just puppets. Jesus, the Man, had an authentic self but it was perfectly and freely keyed in to the will of the Father. In the same way, God wants our wills freely and fully in order that we may become authentic human beings.

The seventh working of the cross is a burden for souls. All evangelism succeeds by prayer. Every soul is ultimately prayed into the kingdom. This is the last stage of intercession where the intercessor, like Moses and Paul, declares his willingness to be damned if only his people might be saved.

All true prayer is identification. Only those who have experienced in their own lives the feeling of alienation from God can really have a hunger and thirst for lost souls. When Jesus cried out on the cross, "My God, my God, why hast thou forsaken me," He was experiencing this utter alienation from God with us and for us.

Many Christians merely witness and evangelize because of enlightened spiritual self-interest. Others seem to be almost totally unconcerned about those ninety-nine out of every hundred who are heading for eternal destruction. The intercessor whose heart is broken for the lost is very close to Him who made intercession for our transgressions on the cross (Isaiah 53:4-9).

As this book comes to a close, the Lord is still revealing truths about intercession. One November I was in Ottawa, Canada, on a mission. The theme was intercession. The Lord had richly blessed the ministry and back in my hotel room I was too tired to sleep. I began to complain to the Lord, "Look, I've done so much for You and You've answered my prayers for others; why don't You answer this tiny little personal prayer I've been praying day and night for two years?"

The answer came, crystal clear, "The intercessor can claim nothing for himself. Jesus was not allowed to turn stones into bread or come down from the cross. Besides, you're claiming the wrong things. The anointing, the gifts and the ministry which I have given you are all from Me. You are a totally undeserving earthen vessel whom I have called, even before you were born. You, my anointed one, are a Pharisee!"

"Truth, Lord, but I claim Your mercy and Your Word," I answered, because suddenly everything had come into focus. I had been approaching God in the wrong way.

It was in February of 1976 in Chicago. Again I was on a mission which the Lord was marvelously blessing. Dead tired, I stumbled into bed at 1:00 A.M. At 4:00 I woke and couldn't go back to sleep. I started to pray for a former neighbor in Brooklyn, dying of cancer. "Lord, don't take her, take me; I'm ready to go but she isn't."

"Don't pray that prayer again; I've warned you twice before. I don't want your life!" The voice was clear and distinct.

"All right, Lord, I've always suspected that You

143

didn't really want me, anyhow," I answered, filled with self-pity.

"Why do you offer your life for all these people, some of whom you don't even know or love? Why don't you offer it to Me instead? All of it!"

"You know, Lord, it's funny I never thought of that. Here, take all of it freely and fully, with no strings attached. No deals, God, and no holding back, no matter what the cost may be. As You have freely given, so I freely give as a love offering. Take me, all of me, as a living sacrifice."

What a glorious release! It was like a new filling of the Holy Spirit. This was what He had been leading up to the whole time.

The story goes on. I pray that it never ends. In 1976 I conducted a retreat near Camp David, Maryland. It was obvious from the very beginning that the Lord had set the whole thing up in advance. I wasn't supposed to go; I didn't really want to go; and some of the people were afraid of me.

The Rev. Norman Smith, a fellow Missouri Synod pastor, was scheduled to lead the retreat. Pastor John Austin of Trinity, my associate, had been asked first but wasn't able to go. At the very last minute the Lord said to me, "Go!"

Starting with Friday night I felt an unusually heavy anointing. Why? I had been on mission the two previous weekends and was totally drained after personally praying for almost a thousand people. I was pushing sixty and the batteries of life were beginning to run down. Serving as associate pastor of a large parish and then going on tour constantly was enough to kill a man half my age.

The anointing began to build up in the forty-odd adults on the retreat. On Saturday night Love Himself walked into the meeting and baptized everyone in the prayer circle, including the pastor. There was joy, weeping and deep love but, in true Lutheran fashion, no wild outward display of emotion.

Sunday morning Pastor Fred Bromal had to be back with his congregation in Glen Burnie. At breakfast a member of his parish, Carol Cavil, inadvertently gave me another word from the Lord.

"Pastor Prange, when you talked about giving yourself to the Lord fully, I realized that I had not been offering Him my life, but my death."

It was like a thunderbolt! That's why God had been saying: "Stop praying that prayer; I don't want your life. Stop offering yourself for perfect strangers; why don't you give yourself to Me."

All the time I had been offering these people and God not my life but my death! I wanted to be rid of my life because I was tired. This was what God was saying, "Give Me your life—not your death." What a glorious breakthrough! From November to February, three fresh anointings of the Spirit! When we break through intercession, the road ahead is clear. It's "go" all the way.

Another strange thing happened at the retreat. The Lord began to show me through Psalm 139 that cutting short even one moment of His eternal plan for us was serious. Lutherans tend to be permissive about smoking, but I had given it up twenty-five years before—strictly "cold turkey." The Lord began to convict the Christians at the retreat about smoking. These are the words He gave based on Psalm 139:

Your eyes saw my unformed substance; every moment and every day were planned (v. 16, free translation). You formed my inner self. You put me together in my mother's womb (v. 13).

145

I have every moment planned for you. There are many that I have ordained to be saved, blessed, loved and healed through you. The last fifteen years of your life are the best. If you deliberately cut them off by chain smoking, you are cheating Me, yourself and your fellow man out of countless temporal and eternal blessings.

These latter words were given to me in the form of prophecy. For twelve years I had stubbornly resisted the "word gifts." This was perhaps the sixth or seventh time I had spoken a prophecy in public.

People everywhere were convicted about smoking. My desk, my bed and my arms were loaded down with packs of cigarets and expensive lighters. We quickly buried them all because some who had renounced smoking began to experience severe withdrawal symptoms. Others had total and complete release after we prayed.

Up until this point I had strongly resisted the Pentecostal concept of a "nicotine demon." Those who had received total and immediate release from the habit of smoking did not have a nicotine or any other kind of demon. But one woman went into a terrible rage after I had buried her cigarets and lighter. We exhausted all the rational and psychological possibilities and finally concluded that there must be something more.

Sunday afternoon, from 1:00 to 2:30 P.M., was set aside for physical healing. There had been healings and other blessings during the communion service in the morning. I anticipated only a handful of people staying. Again, the whole group came forward.

"Lord," I groaned, "what are You doing to me? I'm

exhausted; I want to go home; it's at least a two-hour drive."

"Diffy" didn't want to come to the retreat in the first place. The year before he had been a deacon in the service when I led the retreat at Mar-Lou-Ridge, Maryland. For some reason he was afraid of me. Some began to share Diffy's story with me.

Since 1954 Diffy had been suffering from a rare neurological desease. It started in the left side of his head and then went down through his left eye and face into his throat. Sometimes the pain became so unbearable that he would poke his head through a closet door. The doctors blocked the pain with alcohol injections above his left eye and also removed part of his voice box. The disease and the injections destroyed his left eye, which became completely blind in 1960.

Diffy had been a deeply committed Christian but the pain was too much. He began to rebel against God. He stopped coming to church and twice refused to be prayed for at the retreat. John and George and some of his other friends practically dragged him into the meeting on Sunday afternoon.

Some had been waiting for a long time. I had been putting them off since the day before. Now, as I looked at the sea of expectant faces, I wondered where to begin. Just at that moment John came in with Diffy in tow.

"Pastor, here's two old men who would just like to talk with you. We're stubborn and hard to convince but the Lord just won't quit."

They sat down on the couch near my chair. We opened with a prayer. For some reason I felt moved to begin with Diffy first, even though he had come in last.

We prayed, "Lord Jesus, Great Physician, we know You are here. We can almost reach out and touch Your face. You are so real at this moment. Do what medicine

147

and science have been unable to do. You know the pain that Diffy has endured. It's too much; it's driving him away and not toward You any more.

"By Your blood, sweat and tears, by Your stripes and death, O Lord, have mercy. Touch him right now with the fingers that put the galaxies in place. Speak the same Word that created and upholds the universe. For the power that broke open the tomb on Easter morning, this is nothing."

I touched his face with my hands. Near his left eye I felt a spot of tremendous heat. Underneath my fingers there was movement.

"Jesus, You are touching him now. Jesus, You are praying for him. Jesus, You are healing him now. Glorify Your name! O Lord, I feel Your surgeon's fingers healing, healing!" I heard myself praying. Unseen hands were on my shoulders.

Suddenly, Diffy cried out, "I can see! I can see!"

He took a book and covered his good eye, opened the Bible and began to read with his dead, totally-blind eye. The words are blurred in my memory. It sounded like John 9. "Why was this man born blind?"

I cannot be sure. We were all too stunned to speak or to hear. All around the room there were sobs and cries of praise.

"I've never seen a miracle before," came out of many lips. The others just sat there in a state of shock. It was an eternal moment before God.

Diffy went outside. It was still light and the sun was shining on beautiful Catoctin Mountain. For fifteen years he had only dimly perceived the glories of God's creation. Now he couldn't get his fill of the trees, the rocks and the hills.

"Look," he told John, "I can see all around. I had forgotten how beautiful God's world was, and it isn't even spring. Until you go blind you take all of these things for granted. I'm sorry that I was mad at God. I didn't really believe. I was afraid to be prayed for any more; I couldn't take any more of God's rejection."

Afterwards, when I said good-by, I hugged Diffy. He told me he was going to the doctor the next day. They had planned to schedule an operation to remove the rest of his larynx.

"Diffy," I said, as I looked right into that newly created brown eye, "don't let the doctor talk you out of it." Suddenly I saw that God in His haste had made a mistake—the other eye was blue!

"Pastor, don't worry, no one is going to talk me out of this, I know. I was blind and now I see. My eyes were always a little off-color but the injections of alcohol have made the brown eye even browner. The doctors said that the alcohol would destroy my eye."

"But they didn't say that God would give you a new one," I added. "I wonder what the doctor is going to say tomorrow. Will it blow his mind? If he is wise, he will say, 'Whatever you've been doing, keep on doing it.' "

(The doctors at John's Hopkins Hospital tell Diffy that he cannot see out of his blind eye because it doesn't dilate. Nobody in the history of medicine has seen through such an eye. But Diffy didn't know this, so he kept on seeing anyway.)

After Diffy left we continued to pray for the sick. It seemed suddenly that Jesus Himself was doing the healing. He healed all who came to Him. I just stood by, lent Him my hands and lips and watched. Demons were cast out with loud cries. I found out that there was a nicotine demon. He made an awful racket when he came out of the woman going through "cold turkey."

At Summit Lake after we had prayed for all who came forward, a tremendous peace filled the room. I sat back in my chair and rested in the Lord. There was silence and light. Nobody moved. We were on the moun-

149

tain top and didn't want to come down. But it was time to go back down to the plain and perhaps even to the bottom of the valley.

As I drove home through the beautiful Maryland countryside from Camp David to Frederick and then on I-70 to Baltimore, "there came throughout my earthly dress, great shoots of everlastingness." The Lord was saying plainly, "The last fifteen years are going to be the greatest; the very best is yet to come."

I know this is true. His hand and His hold is ever firmer over me. Even as He blesses, He also breaks and prunes. He's on the "high road" and the "low road," in the good news and the bad. He's on the mountain and also in the bottom of the valley where the action is. I can't pitch my tent on the mountain top because there is much to be done down on the plain. But the valleys are being raised higher and higher.

Even the deepest valleys now seem like mountain tops because even in the darkness of despair, He is there beside me. I can always reach out and touch His hand. I know it's His because there is a nail hole right in the center of it.

As I write these final words, my eyes are filled with tears and my heart is full of joy and praise. When I wrote about Diffy, it was so real that I began to weep even though I'm not the emotional type. At the moment I'm tingling from head to foot with the glory of the Lord. When I look in the mirror I see an aging, homely face, a balding, graying head. Set in the midst of this face are the windows of the soul, eyes out of which the life of Christ shines.

Can a man hide God in his heart? Can we escape from Him? I've tried every way: in the heaven of goodness, in the hell of nothingness, on the wings of the Air Force, in the foxholes of France, in the darkness of the night and the fumes of alcohol. I've even tried to escape from Him in the busyness of the ministry and the crusades of the ghetto. But always His hand finds me out.

There is only one way to escape from God—into His arms, fully and freely. We want to escape from Him because He gets too close and knows too much. But not even death itself can hide us. When we awake, behold we are with Him (Psalm 139:18).

Pray for the anointing on this book and the others which are still to come if He so wills. Somehow I need to share with the world the perfect joy of total surrender to God.

BIBLIOGRAPHY

Allen, Charles. *God's Psychiatry*. Westwood, New Jersey: Revell, 1959.

Bailey, Faith Coxe. *George Muller, Young Rebel in Bristol*. Chicago: Moody Press, 1958.

Barclay, William. *The All-Sufficient Christ*. Philadelphia: Westminister Press, 1963.

—— *The Apostles' Creed for Everyman*, New York: Harper & Row, 1967.

—— *The Beatitudes and the Lord's Prayer for Everyman*. New York: Harper & Row, 1968.

Bisagno, John. *The Power of Positive Praying*. Grand Rapids: Zondervan, 1965.

Bishop, George. *Faith Healing—God or Fraud*. Los Angeles: Bishop-Sherbourne Press, 1967.

153

Bonhoeffer, Dietrich. *The Cost of Discipleship*. New York: MacMillan, 1967.

—— *Life Together*. New York: Harper & Row, 1954.

Buttrick, George Arthur. *God, Pain and Evil*. New York: Abingdon Press, 1966.

—— *Prayer*. New York: Abingdon Press, 1942.

—— *So We Believe, So We Pray*. New York: Abingdon Press, 1956.

Carrington, W. L., M.D. *Psychology, Religion and Human Need*. Great Neck, New York: Channel Press, 1957.

Clarke, Charles. *Pioneers of Revival*. Plainfield, New Jersey: Logos, 1971.

Cox, David. *Jung and St. Paul*. New York: Association Press, 1959.

deChardin, Pierre Teilhard. *Hymn of the Universe*. New York: Harper & Row, 1961.

Deropp, Robert S. *Drugs and the Mind*. New York: (Evergreen) Grove Press, 1960.

Doninger, Simon, ed. *The Nature of Man*. New York: Harper Brothers, 1962.

Ebeling, Gerhard. *On Prayer, Nine Sermons*. Philadelphia: Fortress Press, 1966.

Feifel, Herman, ed. *The Meaning of Death*. New York: McGraw-Hill, 1959.

Frank, Jerome D. *Persuasion and Healing*. New York: Shocken Books, 1963.

Frost, Robert. *Set My Spirit Free*. Plainfield, New Jersey: Logos, 1973.

Funestan, Arvid. *Psychoanalysis and Christianity*. Rock Island, Illinois: Augustana Book Concern, 1958.

Gasson, Raphael. *The Challenging Counterfeit*. Plainfield, New Jersey: Logos, 1966.

Gillquist, Peter E. *Let's Quit Fighting about the Holy Spirit*. Grand Rapids: Zondervan, 1974.

Gross, Nancy E. *Living with Stress.* New York: McGraw-Hill, 1958.

Grubb, Norman. *C. T. Studd.* Chicago: Moody Press, 1962.

—— *The Deep Things of God.* Ft. Washington, Pennsylvania: Christian Literature Crusade, 1970.

—— *The Law of Faith.* Ft. Washington, Pennsylvania: Christian Literature Crusade, 1947.

—— *The Leap of Faith.* Ft. Washington, Pennsylvania: Christian Literature Crusade, 1962.

—— *The Liberating Secret.* Ft. Washington, Pennsylvania: Christian Literature Crusade, 1971.

—— *Rees Howells, Intercessor.* Ft. Washington, Pennsylvania: Christian Literature Crusade, 1973.

—— *Touching the Invisible.* Ft. Washington, Pennsylvania: Christian Literature Crusade, 1972.

Hallesby, O. *Prayer.* Minneapolis: Augsburg, 1931.

Harper, Michael. *Spiritual Warfare.* Watchung, New Jersey: Charisma Books, 1970.

—— *Walk in the Spirit.* Plainfield, New Jersey: Logos, 1968.

Harrell, Irene Burk. *Miracles through Prayer.* Plainfield, New Jersey: Logos, 1972.

Heiler, Friedrich. *Prayer.* New York: Oxford University Press, 1958.

Heim, Karl. *Christian Faith and Natural Science.* New York: Harper Torch Books, 1957.

—— *The Transformation of the Scientific World View.* New York: Harper & Bros., 1953.

Huegel, F. J. *Prayer's Deeper Secrets.* Minneapolis: Bethany Fellowship, 1959.

Huxley, Aldous. *The Doors of Perception: Heaven and Hell.* New York and Evanston: Harper Colophon Books, Harper & Row, 1954, 55, 56.

Jabay, Earl. *The Kingdom of Self.* Plainfield, New

Jersey: Logos, 1974.

James, William. *The Varieties of Religious Experience.* New York: Random House, 1902.

Jung, C. G. *Psyche and Symbol.* Garden City, New York: Doubleday Anchor, 1958.

—— *Psychology and Religion.* New Haven: Yale University Press, 1938.

—— *Two Essays on Analytical Psychology.* New York: Pantheon Books, 1953.

Kelsey, Morton T. *Encounter with God.* Minneapolis: Bethany Fellowship, 1972.

—— *God Dreams and Revelation.* Minneapolis: Augsburg, 1974.

—— *Healing and Christianity.* New York: Harper & Row, 1973.

—— *Tongue Speaking.* Garden City, New York: Doubleday, 1964.

Kierkegaard, Soren. *The Gospel of Suffering.* Minneapolis: Augsburg, 1948.

Koch, Kurt. *Christian Counseling and Occultism.* Grand Rapids: Kregel, 1972.

Kuhlman, Kathryn. *God Can Do It Again.* Old Tappan, New Jersey: Spire Books, Revell, 1969.

Laubach, Frank C. *Prayer, the Mightiest Force in the World.* Old Tappan, New Jersey: Revell, 1946.

Lawrence, Brother. *The Practice of the Presence of God.* Old Tappan, New Jersey: Spire Books, Revell.

Lewis, C. S. *Miracles.* New York: MacMillan, 1953.

—— *The Problem of Pain.* New York: MacMillan, 1955.

—— *The Screwtape Letters.* New York: MacMillan, 1948.

Lindsey, Hal. *Satan Is Alive and Well on Planet Earth.* Grand Rapids: Zondervan, 1972.

Linn, Louis, M.D. *Psychiatry and Religious Experience.* New York: Random House, 1958.

MacNutt, Francis. *Healing.* Notre Dame: Ave Maria Press, 1974.

McGraw, Francis. *Praying Hyde.* Minneapolis: Dimension Books, Bethany Fellowship, 1970.

Meloon, Wilfred C. *We've Been Robbed.* Plainfield, New Jersey: Logos, 1971.

Menninger, Karl. *Whatever Became of Sin.* New York: Hawthorn Books, 1973.

—— *Man against Himself.* New York: Harcourt, Brace, 1938.

Meyers, John. *Voices from the Edge of Eternity.* Old Tappan, New Jersey: Spire Books, Revell, 1973.

Miller, Basil. *George Muller, Man of Faith and Miracles.* Minneapolis: Dimension Books, Bethany Fellowship, 1941.

—— *John Wesley "I Look upon the World as My Parish."* Minneapolis: Bethany Fellowship, 1966.

Mumford, Bob. *15 Steps Out.* Plainfield, New Jersey: Logos, 1969.

Nee, Watchman. *The Latent Power of the Soul.* New York: Christian Fellowship, 1972.

—— *The Normal Christian Life.* Ft. Washington, Pennsylvania: Christian Literature Crusade, 1963.

—— *Spiritual Reality or Obsession.* New York: Christian Fellowship, 1970.

—— *The Release of the Spirit.* Cloverdale, Indiana: Sure Foundation, 1965.

—— *The Spiritual Man.* New York: Christian Fellowship, 1971.

—— *A Table in the Wilderness.* Ft. Washington, Pennsylvania: Christian Literature Crusade, 1969.

Northridge, W. L. *Disorders of the Emotional and Spiritual Life.* Great Neck, New York: Channel Press, 1961.

O'Connor, Edward D. *The Pentecostal Movement in the Catholic Church.* Notre Dame: Ave Maria Press, 1971.

Pelikan, Jaroslav. (Introduction). *Luther's Works.* St. Louis; Concordia, 1959.

Prenter, Regin. *Spiritus Creator.* Philadelphia: Fortress Press, 1953.

Price, Charles S. *Made Alive.* Plainfield, New Jersey: Logos, 1972.

—— *The Real Faith.* Plainfield, New Jersey: Logos, 1940.

—— *Spiritual and Physical Health.* Plainfield, New Jersey: Logos, 1972.

Prince, Derek. *Shaping History through Prayer and Fasting.* Old Tappan, New Jersey: Revell, 1973.

Rees, Paul S. *Triumphant in Trouble.* Old Tappan, New Jersey: Revell, 1963.

Rinker, Rosalind. *Communicating Love through Prayer.* Grand Rapids: Zondervan, 1966.

Sanford, Agnes. *Behold Your God.* St. Paul: Macalester Park, 1958.

—— *The Healing Light.* St. Paul: Macalester Park, 1972.

—— *The Healing Power of the Bible.* New York: Lippincott, 1969.

—— *Lost Shepherd.* Plainfield, New Jersey: Logos, 1971.

—— *Sealed Orders.* Plainfield, New Jersey: Logos, 1972.

Schaeffer, Francis A. *The God Who Is There.* Downers Grove, Illinois: Inter-Varsity Press, 1968.

Schlink, Basilea. *Repentance—The Joy-Filled Life.* Grand Rapids: Zondervan, 1968.

—— *Ruled by the Spirit.* Minneapolis: Bethany Fellowship, 1969.

Sharpe, William D., M.D. *Medicine and the Ministry*. New York: Appelton-Century, 1966.

Siirala, Aarne. *The Voice of Illness*. Philadelphia: Fortress Press, 1963.

Sinnott, Edmund. *Matter, Mind and Man*. New York: Atheneum, 1962.

Thielicke, Helmut. *Between God and Satan*. Grand Rapids: Eerdmans, 1969.

—— *How To Believe Again*. Philadelphia: Fortress Press, 1972.

—— *Life Can Begin Again*. Philadelphia: Fortress Press, 1963.

—— *The Silence of God*. Grand Rapids: Eerdmans, 1962.

—— *The Waiting Father*. New York: Harper & Row, 1959.

Torrey, R. A. *How To Pray*. New York: Pyramid Books, 1970.

Tournier, Paul. *The Adventure of Living*. New York: Harper & Row, 1965.

—— *A Doctor's Casebook in the Light of the Bible*. New York: Harper & Row, 1966.

—— *Guilt and Grace*. New York: Harper & Row, 1962.

—— *The Healing of Persons*. New York: Harper & Row, 1965.

—— *The Meaning of Persons*. New York: Harper & Row, 1966.

—— *The Person Reborn*. New York: Harper & Row, 1966.

—— *A Place for You*. New York: Harper & Row, 1966.

—— *The Whole Person in a Broken World*. New York: Harper & Row, 1966.

Unknown Author. *The Kneeling Christian*. Grand Rapids: Zondervan, 1971.

Warnke, Mike. *The Satan Seller.* Plainfield, New Jersey: Logos, 1972.

Weatherhead, Leslie. *Psychology, Religion and Healing.* New York: Abingdon, 1957.

White, Anne S. *Healing Adventure.* Plainfield, New Jersey: Logos, 1969.

Wigglesworth, Smith. *Ever Increasing Faith.* New York: New Family Library, 1972.